As seen on FOX News Chicago with Bob Sirott, WCIU's *You and Me in the Morning*, Mark Brown's *Chicago Sun-Times* column, *RedEye*, Metromix, Gapers Block, Chicagoist, the *Chicago Journal*, Pioneer Press, and more!

When the Beat Cop pauses from taking a bite out of crime, he takes a bite out of donuts, polish sausage, fried chicken, enchiladas, and omelettes...

Lake Claremont Press's 2004 award-winner, *The Streets & San Man's Guide to Chicago Eats*, delivered tongue-in-cheek style and food-in-mouth expertise by a certified expert of the City of Chicago's Department of Lunch: streets & sanitation department electrician Dennis Foley.

Now, Sgt. David J. Haynes of the Chicago Police Department, and his partner-in-crime, bloggist Christopher Garlington, want to take on Foley's street-level guide to the best mom-and-pop food bargains in Chicago with their follow-up: *The Beat Cop's Guide to Chicago Eats*. "We're funnier, better-looking, and have the street smarts, girth, and weaponry to meet him in any alley, taqueria, or rib joint."

He's no chef, food writer, or restaurateur. A former marine, Sgt. Haynes has spent the past 15 years dodging bullets and chasing down gang bangers on Chicago's West Side, running Chicago's first ever Homeland Security Task Force, and supervising squads in Chicago's 19th District at Belmont and Western. During those years, one of his most daunting tasks—and indeed one of the most important ones—was to get lunch.

Laugh if you want to. Getting lunch for 20 hungry cops who have been riding around in the freezing Chicago winter or blistering summer heat requires a remarkable degree of diplomacy, grit, and street savvy. Seriously, these folks are armed! They're out there putting their lives on the line hour by hour; and when their stomachs are growling, they're not calling for a Big Mac. They want real food—good food—the kind of food that makes them forget about the mean streets of Chi-Town for half an hour. They want Italian beefs, stuffed pizza, and catfish nuggets; they want ribs, red hots, and pulled pork sandwiches.

Navigating this volatile terrain has become second nature to Sgt. Haynes. His knowledge of local eateries comes hard-earned from years on the beat and years of fierce debate with other cops. Haynes's understanding of the best places to get lunch in Chicago makes for an unprecedented blue-collar guide to the best food in the Windy City. You know we're not talking white tablecloths and Perrier.

The cafes and counters in this book are the places where locals go to get a sandwich. They're the places that cater church suppers. Go to one of these joints and you'll sit shoulder to shoulder with pipe fitters, bricklayers, yardmen, sanitation removal engineers, pimps, organized crime leaders, and cabbies.

And cops. Because first and foremost, this book is about where cops eat. On any given day at any of these restaurants, you'll find yourself eating with some of the 11,000 men and women who help keep our city safe. This book is dedicated to them.

"The idea," says Haynes, "is to get in, get a good meal, and get out before your lunch break ends for under ten bucks." Peppered with outrageous stories from working cops, Chicago cop lore, and even a few recipes, *The Beat Cop's Guide* takes you on a gustatory journey through all five CPD areas, including some of the toughest neighborhoods in the nation.

The Beat Cop's Guide to Chicago Eats comes at a time when Chicagoans really need it. The economy is in a slump like never before. Times are tough. Money is tight. The Beat Cop doesn't just direct you to a great meal for eight bucks--he's secured you your very own police discount. The book retails at $15.95 and includes $34 in coupons. It's almost as lucrative as being buddies with your alderman.

The Beat Cop's Guide to Chicago Eats

By
Sgt. David J. Haynes & Christopher Garlington

First Edition

LAKE CLAREMONT PRESS
Chicago

The Beat Cop's Guide to Chicago Eats
Sgt. David J. Haynes and Christopher Garlington

lcp@lakeclaremont.com
www.lakeclaremont.com

Publisher's Cataloging-In-Publication Data
(Prepared by The Donohue Group, Inc.)

Haynes, David J. (David Joseph), 1968-

 The beat cop's guide to Chicago eats / by David J. Haynes & Christopher Garlington. -- 1st ed.

  p. : ill. ; cm.

 Includes index.
 ISBN: 978-1-893121-72-0

 1. Restaurants--Illinois--Chicago--Guidebooks. 2. Restaurants--Illinois--Chicago Metropolitan Area—Guidebooks. I. Garlington, Christopher. II. Title.

TX907.3.I32 C45 2011
647.95773/11   2009921762
15 14 13 12 11   10 9 8 7 6 5 4 3 2 1

This book is dedicated to all the beat cops in Chicago who've ever been hungry, who've ever suffered the agonizing choice of picking chili or hot dogs; the beat cops who eat greasy chow in their squad cars instead of sitting down at a table because they're more focused on fighting crime than filling their gut; and to every hot dog joint, chicken shack, shrimp shack, and pizza place in all five areas: You are the true taste of Chicago.

Contents

Area 3

Area 4

Area 5

Foreword

By Chief Jim Maurer

James Maurer was a Chicago cop for more than forty years, rising from the rank of cadet in 1964 to that of chief of patrol in 2002, in charge of more than ten thousand sworn police officers and several hundred civilian workers. He has received a solid page worth of accolades and awards for his leadership and service, including two superintendent awards of merit, four department commendations, a D.E.A. commendation, the Illinois State Bar Association's Law Enforcement Man of the Year for 2003, and the recognition he is most proud of: appreciation from the residents of Cabrini Green in 2000 for the remarkable success of "Operation Silent Night," when he and four hundred officers put a peaceful and permanent end to the terrifying gunfire (including the firing of AK-47s and other automatic weapons) erupting there every New Year's Eve.

The most difficult decision any cop makes on a given day is where to eat lunch. Unless there's a major call, as soon as a couple of cops get into their car, this decision could take up the next four hours. They might even stop for a hot dog to tide them over until they figure out the perfect place to take their break.

As the managing deputy commissioner for safety and security at the world's busiest airport with one hundred to five hundred thousand people flowing in and out of Chicago every day, I have ample opportunity to give advice to visitors looking for a place to eat in the city. My advice is the same every time: Ask a cop.

Although the old neighborhood places have changed since I started out, in 1964, at seventeen, as a cadet, one thing remains constant: every neighborhood, every beat, has a place that

1

prepares food that's so good, so perfect, so quick to your table that a cop can't help but eat there. But there's more to some places than just the food. There's the stories.

I remember a couple. Once when two of my partners were having an off-duty drink at Mike's, which was a cop bar on Webster, these two guys walk in. One of them stands by the front door while the other walks back the length of the bar into the restroom. Well, that's a sure sign something's about to suck. This bar is packed with cops, off-duty guys, detectives, on-duty plainclothes, all of them armed, all them instantly aware that these two guys are going to try something. Sure enough, the second guy walks out of the bathroom. They come up with guns. One of them says, "This is a—" He barely gets the words out of his mouth when half the bar opens up on them. Half the guys, the guys in the middle, just ducked for cover. There was a lot of lead in the air. They must've shot those guys fifty times.

Then there were places that were interesting because of where they were and how they had to do business. I used to go to this place in the middle of Cabrini Green, Farmer Brown's. Absolutely the best chicken and ribs anywhere! It was in an old currency exchange shop, so to pay, you put your money in one of those metal drawers because you're separated by bulletproof glass. The guy pulled it in; then he shoved your chicken and ribs into the same drawer and pushed it back out to you. Didn't matter though, because the food was so good.

Cops have always known where to get the best food. Years ago, in some neighborhoods people sold food out of their homes. My partner, Fred Bosse, and I used to frequent a place in the 600 block of North Wood Street. This place had excellent hot dogs and Polish and the proprietor sold it right out of the window on the side of his house.

There was a place in 018 called the Saucy Weenie that served Polish sausages grilled with cheese—nobody cared about nutrition. It was quick. You got it and got out.

Years ago, a lot of the ritzier places, like Chez Paul, liked to have cops around. They didn't want any trouble. So a cop could get seated in the kitchen and have the same $40 steak they were serving in the dining room for five bucks. Of course that was a long time ago and today someone would call that corruption.

But most places where cops eat, there's not going to be any trouble. A cop comes in, he does two things: he takes a look around, gets a feel for who's there; then he sits so he's comfortable, so nobody's behind him. A cop knows where there's trouble. You try to avoid these places because the one part of your day you don't want any interruptions is lunch.

You won't have any trouble from the restaurants listed in this book. Although we could debate from now until the end of time which places they left out and which places they should have left out, the hot dog joints and walk-ups listed by Sgt. Haynes and Mr. Garlington are where cops eat. When you're on a date, when you're trying to impress your boss, when you're on an expense account, by all means get a table at Trotter's. Put yourself on the list at Everest. Go ahead, take your mom out to Lawry's. No harm, no foul. You want to know where to get real food? *Ask a cop.*

Preface

By Christopher Garlington

Let's hear it for the literate sanitation disposal technician!

Dave and I were very excited when Lake Claremont Press tapped us to write the second edition of their popular regional guidebook, *The Street and San Man's Guide to Chicago Eats* by Dennis Foley. I was especially excited since I had spent most of my career in retail management and a significant portion of that as a manager for a large national bookstore chain that sold the *San Man's Guide* by the box load.

There's no greater mark of distinction for a book than for booksellers to keep it on their short list for recommendations. *The Street and San Man's Guide* was one of those books. I used to keep two copies at the information booth to save myself the walk across the store. Every Chicago bookseller thought it was hilarious.

And brilliant! Who better to lead the wary visitor or trepid North Sider to a great-tasting platter of deep-fried catfish nuggets or spicy empanadas than a guy with his nose stuck up the ass end of a garbage truck all day? I can imagine Foley's mind seizing on the tantalizing bouquet of sun-baked spoiled milk and dead cat wafting gently from an overflowing back alley bin and thinking to himself, "You know, nothing goes better with dead cat than a chili cheese dog and some onion rings from so-and-so's."

I can see him now, skulking through the alleys behind his big blue behemoth, paring wines with each dumpster's signature bouquet:

Ah, rotting baloney nestled into a plastic bag full of Chihuahua crap! That would marry nicely with a 2004 Chateauneuf des Papes! Mmmmm! A rain-soaked box of old gym shoes is the perfect foil to a 1997 Chilean Malbec/Syrah!

Heavens, is that a crate full of putrefied cabbage and the steaming remains of a neighborhood shrimp boil from last Thursday?! Quick— get me a bottle of Riesling and some brie!

It was cute. It was ironic. It was a noble effort and for that Dave and I offer the author a solemn half-hearted golf clap and kindly beg him to haul his reeking carcass back to his truck.

Getting lunch advice from a garbage man is like taking fashion tips from a used car salesman. What you want is advice from a guy who spends his time where the food begins, not where it ends up.

Cops spend their days chasing burglars, talking crazy people off the roof, and tazing unruly drunks. That takes a lot of energy. It works up an appetite. After a guy's cuffed and locked up, these cops want one thing and one thing only: grub. They don't want to wait on some microchemical foam whipped up at Trotter's or braised rabbit in a pecan glaze with hand-milled grits over at Blackbird. These guys don't want theater. They want food. Now.

Ed. note: Dennis Foley was an electrician for the Dept. of Streets and Sanitation.

By Sgt. David J. Haynes

Cops and Donuts

Donuts and policemen have always been intertwined. When the news of the day does not provide the nighttime talk-show hosts with enough material, they regularly turn to policeman-donut jokes. There are bumper stickers. There are T-shirts . . .

I've had my fair share of donuts, and your fair share, too. Believe me, I know a lot about donuts. I knew when I began writing a book about food, the first thing mentioned would be donuts. So I figure the best thing is to face it first, take the bull by the horns, so to speak.

Today, not many cops eat donuts regularly. As Generations X and Y fill the ranks of police departments across the country, they bring their own ways with them. Some of these ways include a greater emphasis on fitness; they drink less coffee and more energy drinks; they are more sensitive to jokes about cops and donuts. It doesn't matter: the stereotype is permanent, the joke will continue, and there is nothing they can do about it. Except give a ticket to the driver stupid enough to ask the cop who pulls him over, "Hey officer, where's your donut?"

Coffee: The Force behind the Stereotype

Coffee is the real reason for the cop-donut stereotype. Back in the early days of the twentieth century, the only places police officers could grab coffee quickly on their beats were donut shops, so cops would frequent donut shops to get the coffee to get through long night shifts.

Until about ten years ago, the Chicago Police Department worked on a rotating shift basis. Every twenty-eight days, police officers would switch shifts, working days one month, then afternoons, then midnights. It was tough, and most people needed coffee to get through the first few days of each new shift.

Coffee's help in getting through long shifts is obviously nothing new. In fact, when coffee was discovered in Ethiopia by sheepherders, one of its very first uses was to help Sufis pray through the night.

These days, coffee is on its way out, with soft drinks and energy drinks being the choice of Generations X and Y. It amazes me how many young police officers don't even drink coffee anymore. By the same token, since fitness and eating well are on the minds of so many people, most young police officers don't do donuts.

Living the Stereotype: Chicago Cops Making Donuts

Every morning, Detective Jim Evans and his brother Detective Tom Evans do what a lot of police officers do: they head for Dunkin' Donuts. But when they get there, they do something no other police officer has done before them. They unlock the doors and make the donuts.

Jim and Tom along with their brother Larry are the only police officers in the world to own a Dunkin' Donuts franchise. Jim says he figured, "If you can't beat 'em, join 'em. As long as there are cops, there will be people to buy donuts!

It is seen as something of a joke to the community when people hear of cops owning a donut shop, but it is also a pretty good marketing tool. People come in to see the donut shop run by cops. While they're there, they grab a donut.

Jim, Tom, and Larry are good businessmen. Their customers are amazed that the staff is so polite and professional. Listening to them, one might get the impression they expected someone to take their order like they were getting pulled over for a ticket. *"Hey, whatta youse guys want?"*

Not Dunkin' Donuts

I don't have anything against Dunkin' Donuts but they're taking over and cannibalizing all the tiny indie donut joints that used to be in Chicago. There are only a few indie operators out there and the following list is surely partial. But these are our favorites and deserve recognition for not caving to the double D.

Dunkin' Donuts
(OK, except this one, owned by two cops—see above.)
210 Peterson Rd., Libertyville
  847-680-8008
====================

Calumet Bakery
2510 E. 106th St.
  773-721-3747
www.calumetbakery.com

Dat Donut
1979 W. 111th St.
  773-298-1001
8249 S. Cottage Grove Ave.
  773-723-1002
www.datdonut.com

Dinkel's Bakery
3329 N. Lincoln Ave.
  773-281-7300
www.dinkels.com

Donut Doctor
3342 W. Lawrence Ave.
  773-509-1600

Huck Finn's
3414 S. Archer Ave.
  773-247-5515
6650 S. Pulaski Rd.
  773-581-4285
10501 S. Cicero Ave.
Oak Lawn
  708-499-1112
huckfinnrestaurants.com

Nancy's Rainbow Donuts
3204 W. Lawrence Ave.
  773-509-9970

Swedish Bakery
5348 N. Clark St.
  773-561-8919
www.swedishbakery.com

Tastee Donuts
5129 W. 32nd St.
  708-656-0181

How to Use

The Beat Cop's Guide

Throughout the book, some jargon is used that should be explained. In Chicago the city is divided into twenty-five districts. On TV police departments are usually divided into "precincts," so that's what people expect to hear. We do things differently in Chicago. Each district in Chicago is identified by a three-digit number, such as 015. There are over a hundred units in the police department, each with a number. For example: the numbers 001 to 025 are the patrol districts; the police academy is Unit 124. For police officers, these numbers are like a shorthand map. Cops don't say to each other, "Pardon me, fellow, but I must inform you that I am currently reporting to the oh one five district." We say "Yo, I'm in the fifteenth."

The head of most police departments in the United States is called the "chief." In Chicago, we call him the "superintendent." The head of each bureau is a deputy superintendent. The Chicago Police Department is divided into six bureaus. The head of the Bureau of Patrol is the deputy superintendent of patrol. Each deputy superintendent reports to the superintendent.

This book is divided into five sections corresponding to the five areas of the Chicago Police Department. Each chapter reviews favorite cop joints for that area. In addition, we throw in some extras for you:

▼ C O P   T A L K ▼

A peak into the minds and mouths of cops.

These sidebars highlight interesting stories or locales near the restaurant under review.

Off Duty

These sections introduce you to favorite places cops might enjoy when they have a little more than a half hour.

More secret delicious information from us to you.

These are stories and recommendations by Chicago cops, both working and retired. Except for spelling errors and some names changed for anonymity, these sections appear in the exact words of the officer quoted to preserve each cop's unique voice.

And, don't forget to snag your own police discount at some of these places by using the **Beat Cop Bucks** found at the end of the book (p. 127). Just don't flash any fake badges.

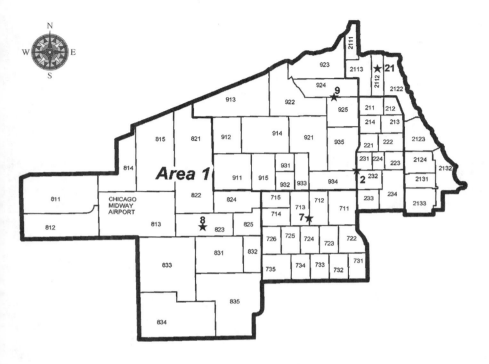

"It is more fun to talk with someone who doesn't use long, difficult words but rather short, easy words like "What about lunch?"
—*Winnie the Pooh*

Mexico Steakhouse

2983 S. Archer Ave.
773-254-5151
Cuisine: *Mexican*

There are hundreds of great Mexican restaurants in Chicago. The real standouts are run by families, and have one great dish that is truly memorable. At the Mexico Steakhouse, it's the soup.

I first went to the Mexico Steakhouse when I was helping to set up an anti-terrorism training course at the Chicago Police Academy. My boss took me there to explain how to better deal with a recalcitrant subordinate.

"Dave, you gotta twist their arm behind their back and get the cuffs on 'em quick. Show 'em who's boss. Otherwise, they could take your gun and blow your brains into the next room. The soup here is good."

I'd never ordered soup at a Mexican restaurant before, being a taco and burrito man, but I decided it would make me look like more of a team player. I had just decided to order it when the waitress brought some, and I found out that you always get soup at the Mexico Steakhouse.

Since then, I've had Mexican soup at other places, and the Mexico Steakhouse follows the same style, but their soup is the best. Like most Mexican joints, the Mexico Steakhouse serves chicken broth with large chicken chunks and vegetables.

Mexico Steakhouse is close enough to downtown to get there quickly. The service is fast. You'll be out and well fed before you have to clock in. Besides soup, there's the usual tacos and burritos, but they're not called the Mexico Steakhouse for nothing. Try the *carne asada*. Seriously, this is a great dish: marinated, roasted flank steak, tender, pounded thin, with crispy edges, served with thick avocado wedges, cilantro, and seasoning.

The prices are right, and the staff is really nice.

▼COP TALK▼

In the Chicago Police Department, the duty day begins at 0001 hours, or midnight. Therefore, midnight to 0800 (8:00 a.m.) is first watch, 0800-1600 (4:00 p.m.) is second watch, and 1600-2400 (midnight) is third watch. We use the term *watch* instead of *shift*.

Tio Luis Tacos
3856 S. Archer Ave.
773-843-0098
tioluistacos.com
Cuisine: *tacos*

The *Tribune* got it right in 2006 when they voted them the city's best tacos. Tio Luis is a true neighborhood joint, squeezed in between two slat board houses on Archer and coming right up to the curb. If you're a tourist, you'll probably drive right by it, but if you're a cop in Brighton Park and you're hungry and you're within driving distance (like in Utah or outer space), this is where you eat.

The steak tacos at Tio's are out of this world. Let me be specific: the *cecina* (dried steak) tacos on the softest, most delicious corn tortillas, cooked in spices and loaded with jalapeños and onions, with just a little extra nudge on the cilantro, these, my friend, are worth taking a bullet for.

I have to mention the rice at Tio's because you might find it a little different from the fluffy, easy on the tongue rice you're used to. Tio's makes traditional Latino rice with a slight tooth, like an al dente rice, with tiny diced potatoes in the mix. The spice is the same damn caliente stuff every Mexican café from here to Caracas drizzles on their mix, but Tio does something to it that

Jalapeño Poppers

One night I took my wife to Uncle Julio's Hacienda. It's not reviewed in this book, because I didn't like it that much. The margaritas were good, but the food was too bland. Except for the appetizer. It was shrimp and jalapeños and cheese enrobed in bacon and roasted to perfection. After that dinner I went home and experimented and came up with a cheaper version that's still a hit at barbeques.

A very important word of caution to guys: once the preparations for this desert have been completed, you cannot scratch the family jewels until the next day, even if you wash your hands. It's painful. Trust me, really, really painful. For what seems like a very long time. And by the way, if you fail to heed my warning, keep it to yourself. The concern and empathy for which women are known completely breaks down when your gonads are burning. All you'll hear are giggles, guffaws, and belly laughs from the one person you expected to have sympathy. Then they'll post it on Facebook.

Having said that, here is the latest version of this recipe. Experiment as you see fit.

12 medium-size jalapeños
1 pound Oscar Mayer bacon
1 package cream cheese
1 can baby shrimp

Cut jalapeños in half the long way and clean the seeds out. The seeds have most of the heat, so the more you leave in, the hotter they are. Put some shrimp in the peppers and cover with cream cheese. Wrap with bacon. Roast on a grill until the bacon is crispy. Remove from grill and serve.

makes it unique. Irresistible.

If you're feeling adventurous, get the horchata. A traditional Latin American drink made from rice, a horchata is milky and sweet. It's a perfect balance for a spicy taco, and if you've just discovered that raw jalapeños are a LOT hotter than you ever dreamed, just grab a glass (or twelve) of horchata. Drink it *slowly*.

This is one of the restaurants where you're very likely to eat with cops, so remember to chew your food, keep the salad fork on the far left, and sip, don't slurp, the soup.

You can get in, get a steak taco the size of my head with beans, rice, and a drink, and get out for under eight bucks.

New China Tea
4024 W. 55th St.
773-284-2463
Cuisine: *Chinese*

They used to be called Hoe Chine Tea. Except for the name, nothing else has changed since before I was even on the force. The food here is standard Chinese, but really, really good standard Chinese. Like Tio Luis, above, the menu looks the same as any of the other joints exactly like it all over the city. You're not going to be stepping out into new culinary territory. Hell, Chinese food's been around so long, I don't even think you can consider it ethnic cuisine anymore. I can walk into this place and order with eyes closed.

But the food, it's good. It's very good. It's really, really good. It's good enough that the place is packed with cops. I don't know how many of these guys work in 008, but there can't be much crime there since the place has about nine thousand cops on any given lunch hour.

A word of warning, a gentle caveat, if you will: the parking here, as in most of Chicago, she is hard. As you're easing into that handicapped space you don't deserve or sneaking up against that fire hydrant, you might be thinking you can get in, grab an egg roll, and get out before you get a ticket. While you're in there, there's a hungry cop looking for a space to eat lunch too, and he will not be entertained by your artistic vehicular placement.

Kapeekoo
6336 S. Pulaski Rd.
773-284-9400
www.kapeekoo.com
Cuisine: *Puerto Rican soul*

You have to love a place that sells great *mofongo*. Kapeekoo bills itself as *cocina Caribena* (Caribbean cuisine), but don't be fooled. This is Puerto Rican soul food.

Some of the dishes are, technically, originally not Puerto Rican, like *mofongo*, which is Dominican (via Africa). But that's a snooty technicality and doesn't matter at all about three nanoseconds after your teeth sink into one of these delicious hush-puppy-esque balls of fried plantanos and pork cracklins.

Don't confuse cracklins with chicharróns. Chicharróns are pretty much the same as pork rinds. Cracklins are different. Cracklins are hot pan and grease derived nuggets of pig flesh, wonderfully rendered of most of their fat until just the meat, salty and firm, is cradled in a crispy manger of fried lard. They're just slightly chewy and they're just slightly salty, and you can't get them enough on the North Side, let me tell you. Imagine the best part of a piece of bacon, but bigger, and spicier. Now imagine it folded into the warm embrace of plantains and spices, rolled into a ball, and deep fried.

It's like Alabama and Cuba had a baby.

Back in the Kapeekoo kitchen, there's no cook. There's a chef: Esmeralda Melendez, and this restaurant is her dream come true.

Historic Pullman Foundation Visitor Center
11141 S. Cottage Grove Ave.
773-785-8901 http://www.pullmanil.org

Less than a mile east of Old Fashioned Donuts is the Historic Pullman Foundation Visitor Center. Although in itself Pullman's history is interesting, the sad story of the company's secretary, Charles Angell, remains one of the most compelling stories of heartbreak and nervous breakdown on record.

As secretary of the Pullman Palace Car Company, Angell had money and prestige. Around 1873, he married one of Chicago's early queens, Eva Badger. Badger was gorgeous, rich, and connected. She was well known in the growing city, a kind of local celebrity. When Mrs. Angell and one of the twins she carried died in childbirth two years later, Angell was inconsolable and friends were worried he might suffer a nervous breakdown. By 1878 Angell had apparently recovered enough to propose again but was refused and sank into a life of despair. There is some indication that Angell tried to forget his troubles in the company of a local prostitute.

It must not have worked. In July of 1878, Angell withdrew some traveling money and walked out of the office. Unknown to the office, Angell had stolen $50,000 in checks and $70,000 in securities, all of which he cashed in New York before disappearing.

When George Pullman returned from his travels and found out about Angell's embezzlement, he put the company resources to work trying to locate the man in the U.S. One hundred thousand wanted posters were circulated throughout the states and around the world. Twenty years after the crime occurred, Angell was found by local police in Lisbon, pretending to be a British citizen named Seymour. He was arrested and returned to the states where he was sent to Joliet.

To put this in a little perspective, the Pullman Company was similar to, say Virgin Airways. If Angell had embezzled the money in twenty-first century dollars, he'd be sitting on top of $31,628,525.31.

You can taste that drive for greatness in her food, which tastes like she's been cooking longer than she's actually been alive. I strongly recommend you eat here now before it gets like some of the more famous Loop joints that need a three-week lead to get a table.

The prices are a little higher than most of the places in this book and I'm not convinced I could get out of there in a half hour. But the food is so good I'll risk it.

Uncle John's
337 E. 69th St.
773-892-1233
Cuisine: *barbeque*

How do you determine who makes the best ribs in Chicago? How can you possibly taste every rib at every joint in the city? Every restaurant sells ribs and everybody claims theirs are the best. The only thing you can do is break it down by neighborhood and let them fight it out at street level.

Or you can eat at Uncle John's.

Here's how good their ribs are: I can't eat ribs anywhere else now. I will, I have, but I don't really enjoy it. I drink Uncle John's sauce *straight*. It's just that good. It's the kind of ribs that make you lose your manners, stick the whole rib in your mouth, and pull the bone out clean. In front of your grandma.

I will declare here and now that Uncle John's makes the best ribs in Chicago—perhaps in the entire world. They sell their rub by the box, but don't think it's going to help you recreate this ruby red masterpiece at home. You can't. It's some kind of magic, some kind of unholy power over pork and beef, some kind of smoker-pit-voodoo that only occurs at this take-out joint. Last time I was there I was in line behind God. *That's how good this place is.*

Make sure you get the hot links. Yeah, a slab of ribs and a plate of hot links. What, are you on a diet or something? Uncle John's hot links are divine packages of perfectly crumbled seasoned pork, cooked so they have that crisp tooth in the first bite; then the inside explodes like a crowd-clearing flash grenade. I ordered two plates to go—one for my fridge and one to eat in the car on the way home. You will convert to porkism after just one serving.

But the best thing about Uncle John's, after the world-conquering food, is the smoke. You might think Uncle John's is run by a guy named John, but it ain't. It's run by a pit boss named Mack. Mack tends the slabs over a smoker that pumps an intoxicating aromatic plume a mile in every direction. It gets into your uniform, it gets into your squad car, and for a while, you smell like ribs. I caught myself smelling my standard-issue white shirt (for *good* reasons) on the highway back from Uncle John's and wondering how I could keep the perfume of mulberry and hickory wood in my car forever. I guess the only thing I can do is go back, fight for a parking space (you've been warned), and roll the windows down.

Remember this is a beat cop's guide for cheap food, not for white tablecloths, so when you go there and find out there's nowhere to sit down, just take a glance at those prices and your worries will vanish. Uncle John's sells ribs so cheap, he must raise the cows in the basement.

You might consider calling ahead as they are incredibly popular—don't be an idiot and show up at 5:00 p.m. and wonder why they're out of ribs. Also, bring a wad of cash. They charge

Drunken Deer Chili

In addition to being a police officer, I am an avid biker. For several years, the biker group that fights against helmet laws in Illinois, A Brotherhood Aimed Toward Education (ABATE), has hosted a chili cook-off at the Park Ridge VFW in February. It's one of the highlights of the biker community during winter.

A few years ago, I found out that if you joined the contest, you didn't have to pay the entrance fee. I figured, "Hey, that's like three more beers," so I entered my chili. My friend Bill (of Bill's Pub on Pulaski) had gotten his deer that year, so I made venison chili.

As a marketing tool, I added Jack Daniel's. When you cook the chili in the crock pot, the alcohol evaporates, so I knew it was safe. I thought that when I put the name on it, and people heard the whiskey was in it, it would win me points with the judges. I was surprised as anyone when the Jack added a really cool smoky flavor to it.

I haven't won yet, but I keep trying. Last time, some guy who put chocolate in his chili won. I can't understand that.

The great thing about any chili recipe is that it can be tweaked. Take this recipe and change it if you wish. Mine always changes a little. For instance, I list beans as optional. I used to always put beans in until a certain member of my household developed into a competitive flatulator–professional level.

> **1 ½ pounds venison meat (very small cubes)**
> **1 ½ pounds beef (very small cubes)**
> **1 pound ground beef**
> **6 jalapeño peppers (seeded and chopped)**
> **1 diced green pepper**
> **1 diced red pepper**
> **1 diced yellow pepper**
> **1 chopped Vidalia onion**
> **2 cloves garlic, sliced**
> **1 cup Jack Daniel's sour mash whiskey**
> **2 cans chili beans (optional)**
> **5 tablespoons chili powder**
> **Salt, pepper, oregano to taste.**

Brown all the meat. Sauté onion and garlic briefly in olive oil, just long enough to heat through. Mix all ingredients except 2 tablespoons chili powder, salt, pepper, and oregano in a crock pot and cook on its lowest setting for 8 hours. After 8 hours add rest of chili powder and spices to taste. Cook 2 more hours and serve with cheese crackers and beer.

like it's 1958 because they actually think it's 1958 and they don't take plastic.

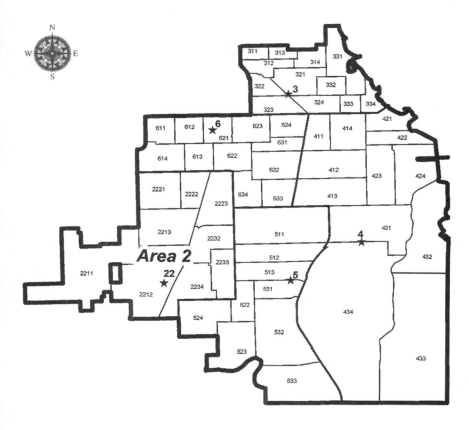

"Donuts. Is there anything they can't do?"
—Matt Groening, *The Simpsons*

Area 2

Eat & Run

1733 W. 87th St.
773-429-1812
www.eatandrunchicken.com
Cuisine: *fish, barbeque, chicken*

It's not just another fish and chicken place on the South Side. It's the Eat & Run, home of the General and his mottos:

"Chicken for Churches but Not Church's Chicken (You Know What I Mean)"

"As Good as Your Mother's and Better Than Others!"

Eat & Run's true to its name—except it's more like "run in and eat." They do a lot of pickup and a lot of catering. They really do make the perfect after-church meal: fried chicken, potato salad, slaw, green beans, and peach cobbler.

But the Eat & Run is best for dashing in and knocking back a quick lunch that tastes like God's mom made it.

Not a lot of people review coleslaw. I guess it gets a backseat to main courses because I just don't see it mentioned much, but the General's coleslaw deserves a word.

Coleslaw should never be a knock-off side. It's a noble and complex dish that needs a delicate touch to make it sing. The cabbage has to be *shaved* into threads; then tossed with fresh mayonnaise. These threads have to achieve a perfect color balance of the creamy pale inner leaves and the bright green outer ones—it must appeal to the eye as well as the tongue. It should have a little zip (cayenne pepper can't hurt) but still balance the main course.

The slaw at Eat & Run is clearly some kind of unwritten family recipe that exceeds those qualifications. It is a delicious, crunchy, zesty foil to their signature chicken and, even better, their unique catfish nuggets. You can't get them anywhere else.

And they love cops! The Eat & Run treats uniforms like the respected members of the community they are. And I'm not saying they treat cops better than your average citizen, just that my platters of chicken and fish are awfully heavy . . .

Bangkok Thai 55

451 W. 31st St.

312-326-5819

Cuisine: *mysterious, Thai*

We include BT55 for sheer weirdness. They are cheap and they're in a neighborhood that has a lot of cops, especially when the Sox are playing. But if what you're looking for is a fine dining experience with, like, lights and a clean floor, look elsewhere.

However, there's something to be said for blasé inconsistency. It's kind of like they don't really give a crap. You may or may not get exactly what you ordered (I suggest you pronounce it "BEEEEF" to be sure you don't get chicken) and they may or may not be open between 11:00 a.m. and 10:00 p.m. as their sign boldly claims. You won't know until you *ring the buzzer to get in.* And then it might be takeout only, even though that's supposed to be only on Sundays. I've been there twice and they got my order wrong both times. The food was good enough—though I still don't know what the hell makes their Thai food Thai food. In the case of BT55, I'm betting that the inclusion of the word *Thai* in the name has more to do with the flavor of the cuisine than any actual ingredients. It tasted like typical Chinese takeout—and not the good kind.

So why include it at all? Because it's just weird, man, and

StreetWise

My partner and I, homicide dicks from Area 2, spent five years on midnights in the late '90s. There was a lot going on in Area 2 to keep a couple of homicide dicks occupied, but not much in the way of good eats at 2:00 a.m. We would often head to Chinatown to Yee Hung on Cermak. When the weather was warm, we would take our orders (mine was always a large beef fried rice, spicy, with an egg roll, and we would go up to the Rush Street area for some late night sightseeing. On one particular night we were sitting along the curb, enjoying our lunches, watching the world pass us by when a particularly stunning, long-legged beauty in a short skirt greeted us as she walked by. "Hello officers," she said. She then continued down the sidewalk, and as she got in front of our car, she deftly lifted the back of her skirt up, revealing a beautifully shaped, pantiless derriere. I almost choked on my egg roll!

Another time, in the late '80s I was working a beat car in Gresham (006). Earlier in the evening my partner and I stopped at a Chinese restaurant on 79th and Aberdeen. As usual I got the fried rice. We took our meals back to the station and ate our lunches there. Later that evening we responded to a burglar alarm at this same establishment. The place was closed and no one was around. We went around the back and saw that the rear door was ajar. Entering into the back and walking into the kitchen, the first thing I saw was three large piles of cooked white rice on the counter. Each pile was approximately the size of a beach ball. Also out on the counter were several dozen eggs. This struck me as being somewhat unhealthy and a made a mental note not to get fried rice from this establishment in the future. However, the thing that turned me off the most was the three cats that were walking on the counter, through the rice, and eating the rice. Not that I had any complaints about my earlier meal, but . . .
—*P.O. Patrick Durkin, Unit 620*

sometimes that counts. Sometimes your dinner should be a kind of gamble, a roll of the dice. Like punching D-11 for Skittles and instead getting a Twinkie from 1976. I mean, sometimes you just have to go for it.

I have a good friend who spends a month every year in Thailand for, um, recreational purposes, and the way he tells it, the sheer randomness of BT55 is right on target. When you're on patrol and cruising around in your black and white and realizing that, hey, most crime happens at night and there's no Sox game and nothing on the radio and your partner is exhibiting all the erudition and zeal of a fresh corpse, you realize you need a little adventure. A gamble.

And, truthfully, it comes down to a dude thing. You and your partner are bored and hungry and you say "Dude—Bangkok 55!" and a lasting gustatory adventure is born.

Steak & Egger
1174 W. Cermak Rd.
312-226-5444
Cuisine: *steak, eggs*

Look. I'm a cop. I know what you're doing at three in the morning out with your buds in your car so I'm going to give you some advice. If you're anywhere near Cicero, go to the Steak & Egger and lay some serious biscuits and gravy on that tank full of cosmos you're driving around on.

The Steak & Egger couldn't be more aptly named. Look, it's a machine. You're gonna get steak. You're gonna get eggs. That should be pretty clear from the sign. I don't even know why they have a menu—you should just walk up and hand them your money and they hand you a plate of steak. And eggs.

But they do try. Besides the obvious (chopped rib eye and eggs, $6.95) they have hash and eggers, pork and eggers, bacon and

 ## Parking Lot of the Steak & Egger

The Chicago Outfit are nothing if not capable businessmen and being in prison is simply no excuse for not earning. When the feds were cracking down on illegal video poker back in the late nineties and early twenty-first century, they were so hot on the heels of the men working ENTIRELY LEGITIMATELY for James "Jimmy the Man" Marcello, the men were forced to hold ENTIRELY LEGAL BUSINESS meetings in the parking lot of the Steak & Egger.

Well, only once. But once is enough to gain a permanent place in Chicago mob history.

When Mickey Marcello visited his older brother at Milan prison in May, 2003, the conversation was recorded by the feds. ALLEGEDLY, the REALLY NICE Marcello family owned a PERFECTLY LEGAL video poker business and were eagerly expecting video poker to be legalized outside Illinois. Discussing what would happen when their industry went legit, the younger Marcello apparently indicated that the other companies with poker machines would rake in millions. Jimmy the Man quickly schooled his kid brother: "First us, then them."

Video poker isn't illegal in Illinois and the outfit guys weren't breaking any laws in the installation of PERFECTLY LEGAL video poker machines in about forty bars in and around Chicago. What was illegal was the very enticing cash payouts often made to customers.

A TOTALLY LEGAL video poker machine takes in anywhere from fifty to one hundred thousand bucks a year. One machine. The outfit splits it with the bar owner. It's kind of like an ATM in reverse. In trying to keep tabs on the mob and their ENTIRELY LEGITIMATE business, the feds were taping the crew who met, once, outside the Steak & Egger.

(Mr. Garlington would like to express his sincere appreciation of all the good work done in the community by members of M & M Amusement, a company made up of really, really good people. Seriously. Please don't kill me.)

eggers, ham and eggers—you get the idea.

It ought to be clear by now, after having drooled through this book all the way to the South Side entries that neither myself nor my associate, Mr. Garlington, gives a crap about our hearts and the Steak & Egger proves it with a greasy truck stop swagger. It's one of those places where you can get breakfast any time of day, and true to the nature of South Side cooking, it's drenched in delicious pork fat and butter. They ought to install a defibrillator at every table or have a CPR pictogram slipped into every menu. (I suspect the waitresses have to be trained.)

A typical meal: rib-eye steak and eggs, onion rings, soup, salad, coffee, a chocolate milkshake, and a cardiologist referral. But I'm not saying that's a bad thing. I'm saying that there's a place for places like this place: namely to keep a tired cop going as the sun's about to come up.

Ken Tone's Drive-In
551 W. 18th St.
312-226-4004
Cuisine: *burgers, sandwiches*

They're cheap, they're damn good, and their parking lot is always full of cop cars and city trucks. That's a sign of true worth. Ken Tone's is a simple sandwich shop. You can get in, get a burger and fries, get an Italian, get a Polish, and get out for less than eight bucks.

However, true to form for all thriving small-time shops, Ken Tone's knows where the money is, and it ain't in dinner. It's in breakfast and lunch. They're open 6:00 a.m. to 5:00 p.m. Monday through Friday and only till 4:00 p.m. on Saturdays. Sunday? Are you kiddin' me?

Get a BLT and a coke and you're back on patrol for under five bucks.

Taqueria Los Comales

3623 S. Archer Ave.

773-890-4307

www.loscomales.com

Cuisine: *Mexican*

Problem: It's 2:00 a.m. and you're on beat. You're hungry. You don't want another hamburger. You don't want the crappy cold turkey sandwich that's in your lunchbox. You're in Pilsen.

Solution: Los Comales. You know it's good because when you do show up at 2:30 in the morning there's *a line.*

I am a cheap Mexican food snob. I live near one of the greatest Mexican restaurants in the city (Tanzitaro) and I know good, cheap Mexican food. When I tell you Los Comales is the real deal, you have to take my word. There are, literally, seventy-five thousand taco joints in the city of Chicago (I'm including tamale carts) and I've been to most of them—twice. Los Comales puts them all to shame without even trying.

Like its distinguished South Side cousins, soul food joints, taquerias have to meet a few requisites to be good. First, the food has to be perfect. I don't mean it has to be good enough, I mean it has to make you growl with pleasure *while it's still in your mouth.* Los Comales does that. When me and my buddy eat there we sound like two starving dogs.

Secondly, it has to be cheap. Los Comales serves one of the world's greatest tacos (*lengua*—a tongue taco; the kind of delicious food that licks you back) for less than a buck fifty.

My only complaint is the stunning lack of *lomo del rey y nopalitos,* (rib eye with fried baby cactus), one of my favorite Mexican meals.

Great Guacamole á la G

Repeat after me: I will not measure.

Look, this is easy. Get a bunch of avocados. You pick up a nice dark green fruit that looks like a dinosaur egg. Now, gently press the fruit near the stem, on the little shoulder of the fruit. If it gives a little—just a little—then this is a nice fatty avocado. If it feels like an actual petrified dinosaur egg throw it back. If it cracks or there is space between the peel and the meat, throw it back. Get at least two for each person because once they start eating this guac, there's no turning back.

Get a fistful of garlic. Get a lemon. Get a lime. Get some salt. Get some fresh ground pepper.

Get a big bowl. Slice the lemon and lime in half. Hold each half in your hand then jam a fork in it. Squeeze it and keep ramming that fork all around until all the juice and some of the pulp is in the bowl. Now run the garlic through a garlic press until there's a respectable glob of it in the middle of the bottom of the bowl. Grind some pepper into it. Now you're ready.

Slice each avocado in half. Use a spoon to dig out the meat. Be sure to gently scrape out the bright green meat that's right up against the skin. When avocado meat meets oxygen it turns grey. If you see any grey meat, get rid of it.

Now, get a fork and mash that stuff into a chunky pulp. How chunky? You're asking me? Mix it up real good, make sure you get all the garlic and stuff in there. Taste it. Salt it. Pepper it. Mix it again. Now, smooth it all down and draw some swirls in the top with the tines of your fork and serve it.

There won't be any left because this is the world's greatest guacamole. However, should you wish to save some, you may be tempted to leave the seed in the bowl of guac to "keep it green." This is total horse caca. If you want your guac to stay pretty, just lay a film of Saran Wrap right on top. Make sure there are no air bubbles. It doesn't last long so don't even try to store it longer than overnight.

Shark's Fish & Chicken

4048 S. Cottage Grove Ave.

773-538-4889

Cuisine: *seafood, wings, chicken*

Another South Side favorite that's doing good. You can find Shark's Fish & Chicken joints all over the city—like cornmeal-battered oases in a sea of bad cheeseburgers. Shark's is a no-frills kind of place. Fish and chicken joints are a South Side staple and pretty much describe the cuisine as you leave the Loop headed toward Indiana. Shark's deserves special mention for a few reasons.

First of all, I am an aficionado of greasy spoons. I do not share a snobbish disdain for restaurants that couldn't care less if your heart explodes three feet away from their front door. *I love them. I trust them.* I don't care if their menus are dirty, if their TV is always on, or if the plant just inside the door is dead, has always been dead, and will never be alive. I don't care. I'm there for the fried catfish, not the ambience. There is no ambience. There's fish and there's chicken. You want ambience? Go next door to the liquor store, I hear they sell ambience by the quart.

Secondly, the fish at Shark's is not encased in a deep-fried flour armoring like other places. It is lightly and carelessly dredged through cornmeal. So their fish tastes like fish, not like Kentucky Fried Chicken. Shark's fried catfish is delicious. Period. It ain't a wine. It don't present a delicate and nutty nose, with a distinctly golden finish. It's fish. FISH, ya snob! Shut up and eat.

As to service, well, it's kind of hit and miss. And I don't mean just location to location. I mean hour by hour. These people are *cooks*, they have a *job* to do. They serve something like eighteen tons of fried catfish every *day*. Give them your order, pay them their money, and walk away.

And, yes, the Cottage Grove Avenue location *is* next to a liquor store and a bus stop so you can get off, get some chicken, get some ripple, and be back on the bus in less than fifteen minutes.

Shark's is located just outside the neighborhood that was listed as the second most violent in the nation in a 2008 *Chicago Sun-Times* story. In Chicago, we don't think much about it. Cops spend most of their time in violent neighborhoods. It's not something we dwell on. However, what makes Shark's interesting is that in addition to being located near one of the worst neighborhoods, it's only a few blocks away from President Obama's house. That's the Chicago way. Our neighborhoods are enclaves, worlds unto themselves. People don't care about what's beyond the bounds of their neighborhoods.

John Powers said in *The Last Catholic in America* that kids in Chicago believe the world ends just beyond their neighborhoods. Their parents are pretty sure that it extends a few blocks more. I remember growing up and not being able to imagine that there was anything beyond Wrigley Field to the east, the river on the west, Welles Park and Montrose to the north, and a block or two beyond Addison to the south.

Even now, when the world is connected by cell phones and the Web, we still tend to spend most of our time in our own neighborhoods.

Shark's is equidistant between the house of "The Most Powerful Man in the World" and some of the toughest gangbangers in the city. If you eat there, you just might see both.

Punky's Pizza & Pasta
2600 S. Wallace St.
312-842-2100
Cuisine: *Italian, pizza, sandwiches*

White Sox game staple. You go to a White Sox game, you go to Punky's and get a hoagie. They're nice. They're cheap. They make good food. What else you want?

There's a million little neighborhood places like Punky's all over Chicago. The important questions for a place like Punky's are:

a) Do they have gyros?

b) Do they serve pizza by the slice?

Punky's is a decided no on gyros, though they do offer a Greek salad so go figure. But they serve pizza by the slice, which is important since there's no room for a pizza box in a squad car. Unless you get the guy handcuffed in the backseat to hold it.

Punky's ain't much to look at, but the great places rarely are. People on the South Side swear by their pizza and the Italian dishes are *ginormous*.

Harold's Chicken Shack
7310 S. Halsted St.

773-723-9006

www.haroldschicken.com

Cuisine: *seafood, wings, chicken*

Harold's Chicken is one of those Chicago South Side joints that made it good. How good? They've got ninety-four stores. They're a regional success story. They have their own Wikipedia page. The chicken is terrific—beaks and neck bones above every chicken shack you've ever seen advertised on TV (rhymes with Flentucky Flide Flickin . . .), but I'm not convinced it's the fried chicken that got them famous. I think it's the fried chicken *livers and gizzards*.

Soul food is one of those cuisines born from the frugality of desperate housewives who not only believed that the maxim of "waste not, want not" was a sign of good character and thrift, it also showed them the way to feed seven people on a budget for five. You just throw in the gizzards. (What other cuisine offers deep-fried bass cheeks and pickled pig's feet?) Harold's stays true to soul food dictums by serving livers and gizzards and, as my friend, the displaced southern expat, can tell you, they are delicious. There's nothing like them. Don't let the fact that chicken gizzards also make really good catfish bait get to you. They're good. Eat one.

Old Fashioned Donuts
11248 S. Michigan Ave.
773-995-7420
Cuisine: *donuts*

Jesus, Mary, and Joseph. Despite my attempt to dissuade you from maintaining the egregious connection between cops and donuts, I will now plunge wholeheartedly into that vat of political incorrectness and wallow in it. *These are the best donuts in the world.*

Old Fashioned Donuts has been making these little halos of dough since I was in grade school and probably longer. They have a following that borders on cultish and it's easy to taste why: biting into one of their fritters for the first time will change your life. They are sublime. They are the epitome of all things donutic. They deserve landmark status as far as I am concerned. Yeah, yeah, yeah, they have Polishes and other food and yeah, yeah, yeah it's all good. *Whatever.* You don't go to Donut Paradise for the hot dogs. You go for the donuts.

It's important to realize that this establishment is the exception that proves the rule: if cops really were genetically predisposed to eating donuts, there'd be a line of blue uniforms stretching from Old Fashioned Donuts all the way to Indiana.

▼ COP TALK ▼
Desk: at every police station in the city of Chicago, there is a desk manned twenty-four hours a day by a sergeant and several police officers who take reports and process prisoners. In my opinion, the desk is one of the hardest jobs in the department. Imagine, if you will, that when you go

to work you're handed the keys to a car with a full tank of gas and told to go hang out for a while. It's a lot of fun. Even when it's busy it's almost always interesting. However, at the desk, you're stuck. There is all of the bad that goes along with the job-complaints, reports, etc.-and none of the good. Nobody smiles and waves, no little kids look up to you at the desk. Just bad guys and people with problems.

Tropic Island Jerk Chicken
419 E. 79th St.
773-224-7766
Cuisine: *Caribbean*

The farther away from the poles you travel, the spicier the food gets until somewhere around the equatorial line, you reach spice nirvana and everything from donuts to dark coffee is laced with something to give it a little kick. The Caribbean method of flavoring meat—from fish to farmyard friends—is called jerk and they've been doing it in the islands since 1655 when the first African slaves were dumped onto Jamaican shores.

Like any great food, jerk comes from the concentrated and gifted efforts of millions of slaves, poverty-stricken moms, and dirt-poor backyard barbeque aficionados trying to make the best out of what they're left with.

For the slaves, this meant chicken and whatever was growing nearby. Fortunately for the rest of the world, Jamaica and the surrounding islands are lush with spices, fruit, and sugarcane and over several centuries there has emerged from the kettles of countless kitchens a complex sauce that turns cheap chicken (pork, fish, whatever you have, even yak) into the food of the gods. You can test this theory by dropping in at the Tropic Island Jerk Chicken grill where you will pay less than eight bucks for red beans and rice and two sides (mac-n-cheese, yams, plantains, mixed greens, green beans, garlic potatoes, stir-fry corn, fresh salad, or steamed cabbage), and jerk chicken, catfish, or shrimp. They also have a slew of Caribbean staples including truly delicious curry goat, oxtail soup, and callaloo.

I will not attempt to describe callaloo except to say that it is a green, like collards or turnip but . . . different. I am an adventurous *gustateur*, a global glutton, so my tastes are broad, egalitarian, and sure to scare the bejesus out of most people. I love callaloo but it is a preciously local dish, born of the necessities of living in island nations, and it is not for everybody. If you're the kind of person who easily eats sweetbreads, tripe, chitlins, fried baby cactuses, or curried goat, then by all means order the callaloo. Otherwise, stick with the wings and the jerk chicken.

My friend the southerner lived a long time in Florida where Caribbean cuisine is prevalent. (He's told me stories about eating jerk catfish cooked on fifty-gallon-drum grills off the side of the road). He says Tropic Island is the real deal. The clincher is the Kola Champagne, a delicious (non-alcoholic) soda that's not exactly a cream soda and not exactly a vanilla coke. I know they can't take credit for making the stuff, but the fact that Tropic Island serves it is a badge of authenticity that deserves note.

Tropic Island is one of those disappearing kinds of places with no seating at all. Not even stools. You line up and pay at a window, get your food through a slot, then walk away and tear into the divine chow as if you haven't eaten in twenty years. Then, if you're anything like me, you get back in line.

Original Rainbow Cone

9233 S. Western Ave.

773-238-7075

www.rainbowcone.com

Cuisine: *dessert, lunch, party*

For more than eighty-two years this family-owned South Side ice cream joint's been serving homemade ice cream cones the size of your head. Yes, I said HOMEMADE. This is not diet food. Neither is their rainbow cake, their caramel apples, or their pulled pork.

Let me reiterate: homemade ice cream, rainbow cake, and pulled pork sandwiches. It's like dying and going to diabetic heaven.

The city literally grew up around this shop, which once stood alone in the midst of dirt roads and open fields in a location considered so remote they called the place the Lodge.

You know they're good because some days the line stretches around the corner of the building. Get in line, get a cone. Don't tell your friend Jenny Craig you were there.

To me Rainbow Cone is not a restaurant; it's a booth at the Taste of Chicago. For years, I didn't even know there was an actual restaurant that served the rainbow cones. I grew up believing that it was something that you get once a year when you went to Grant Park for the annual salute to gastronomical indulgence.

The last time I had a cone at the Taste of Chicago, I was working. I was assigned to walk around as part of a tactical team when I was assigned to the 001 District. I was waiting for the rainbow cone I had just ordered when a lovely young lady walked up to me and said, "Excuse me." With what I now realize was an over-inflated ego, I thought she wanted to chat, so I made the mistake of saying, "Yes?"

Two things happened then: The lovely young lady said, "I have a warrant out on my boyfriend, and he's standing right over there." Simultaneously, the lady behind the counter walked up with my rainbow cone, and my hand was halfway to her before my brain realized what I had just been told.

I actually looked at her, then back at the cone, then back to her as if I was watching some kind of philosophical tennis match. Then my professionalism overcame my gluttony and I walked over to where she had pointed, where, sure enough, there was her boyfriend, and sure enough, he had a warrant. The rest of the day was spent in a trailer doing paperwork.

Don't worry, I eventually got my rainbow cone, and it tasted all the better following a healthy dose of justice.

Closed on Mondays.

Pupuseria El Salvador
3557 E. 106th St.
773-374-0490
www.pupuseriaelsalvador.com
Cuisine: *Salvadoran*

This place epitomizes everything this book stands for. They're cheap. They're local. The food is made by gorgeous women and blessed by God Almighty.

They serve pupusas, which taste kind of like a Jamaican meat pie and a taco had a baby. And I can't stress this enough—*they're cheap.* You can stuff yourself on delicious one-of-a-kind Latino food, dig a great local scene, and walk out for less than eight bucks.

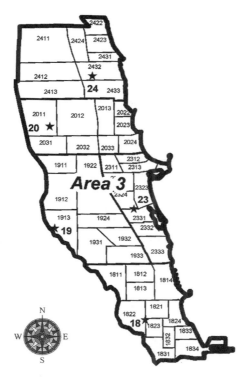

"The History of every major Galactic Civilization tends to pass through three distinct and recognizable phases, those of Survival, Inquiry and Sophistication, otherwise known as the How, Why and Where phases. For instance, the first phase is characterized by the question 'How can we eat?' the second by the question 'Why do we eat?' and the third by the question 'Where shall we have lunch?'"
—Douglas Adams, *The Hitchhiker's Guide to the Galaxy*

StreetWise For cops, trying to eat at a restaurant without being bothered is difficult, which is why most cops learn to dine *en automobilia* (in the car). Even then, the goofs will find you like moths find flames.

Once, while tucked away in a local cemetery with a sandwich and a TV and watching the Bears game, a car pulled up and asked how to get to the exit.

Once, while lunching in the car at Ohio Street Beach at about 5:30 a.m., a jogger ran up to tell us that a fisherman down near Oak Street Beach had asked him to call the police because when he pulled his line out of the water, he discovered a dead body on his hook.

Once, while parked near the Lincoln Park Zoo on Cannon Drive (before it was a parking lot), and around 2:00 a.m., we were enjoying a Dagwood and fries, when a car full of beautiful young women pulled up next to us. They said a car was following them and they thought the driver was drunk. We assured them that we would look around for the drunk driver (wink, wink!), and they pulled away. About five seconds later, their drunken stalker rear-ended the squad car and the carload of women kept right on going and never looked back.

The late Lt. Rex Redstone was a sergeant in 018. When on first watch, he was active on jobs and backups till everything died down about 5:00 a.m. Then he liked to get a cup of joe and a newspaper and relax. He parked at the loading dock of a factory, and between a couple of semitrailers. Just in case he dozed off (he did every night), his guys would know where to find him in an emergency. Sergeants don't go down for lunch on the air, but his trusted guys knew his routine. One night they punked him by having the shifter silently drop a semitrailer in front of the slot where he was parked. He now was boxed in by the shipping dock behind him and trailers in front and on both sides. They got the desk crew to call the sergeant in to see the captain and the fun was on. He couldn't open the car doors nor crawl out the windows to get the front trailer moved. He called for a meet with his guys, and they said they just started eating their lunch and they'd be there in about twenty minutes. This was before those newfangled contraptions known as cell phones, so Rex was ready to piss in his pants.

The POs finally fessed up and all involved had a good laugh. The story is now CPD legend. And it all started from that 5:00 a.m. "lunch." —*Sgt. Kent Erickson, Ret.*

Hero's
3600 N. Western Ave.
773-327-6363
Cuisine: *submarine sandwiches*

In an era of chain submarine sandwich restaurants, Hero's is a throwback. The small white building on the corner of Western and Addison across from Lane Tech doesn't seem to have changed a bit since it opened in 1963. And why should it? None of the new places seems to be able to capture the taste and appeal of this Chicago classic.

Crusty white bread is delivered and cut every day (white bread only, some things are worth being a little unhealthy). The meats and veggies are cut fresh every few hours. The teenagers behind the counter are well trained and extremely efficient, getting hundreds of people in and out of the restaurant during a lunch.

There are no seats. You can stand at the window counter and stare at the traffic whizzing by three feet away on Addison while you pray that no one loses control of their car and smashes into the restaurant before you finish your hoagie.

Luckily, a lot of city workers eat there and they leave their big city trucks in the right lane of traffic to act as a barricade. If they're not there, a police officer is probably around, so there will be someone to write a report if the worst happens, and the high schoolers from Lane will help by cheering if someone gets hurt. The cool pictures of Bears and Bulls players round out the décor.

When I attended Lane Tech, Hero's was a popular location for lunch, and it still is. I notice now when I eat at Hero's, I run into people who tell the owner they used to eat there when they were kids.

Hero's only accepts cash. No debit cards or credit cards. However, they recently installed an ATM. So people like me who try not to carry cash don't have to walk across the street.

Art of Pizza

3033 N. Ashland Ave.
773-327-5600
Cuisine: *pizza*

Pizza raised to a fine art. In a city of good pizza, the Art of Pizza stands out. The pizza is really good, and that should be enough, but what makes the Art of Pizza different is that the pizza can be bought by the slice. Most of the pizza places I go to either have a bunch of appetizers, great pizza that they don't sell by the slice, or pizza by the slice that's not that great. I'm a sergeant in a squad car supervising a whole section of cops and detectives. I'm busy. I don't want to order a whole pizza to eat by myself, so it's great to have a place that sells good pizza by the slice. The prices are reasonable and the place is clean—although the décor is a little cold and without personality. Kind of like some detectives I know.

Next door to the Art of Pizza is a place called the School of Rock. The School of Rock teaches young kids to play musical instruments in the rock-and-roll style. If you have kids, you can sign them up to be rock stars, and then enjoy some pizza while you wait for them.

Chicago Pizza & Oven Grinder Co.

2121 N. Clark St.

773-248-2570

www.chicagopizzaandovengrinder.com

Cuisine: *Italian, pizza, subs*

There are a lot of reasons why I love this place so much: the location; the quaint brick-front three-flat squished up against its neighbor; the people who run it, who are lovely, gregarious, and fun; the food, which is almost indescribably delicious. But one thing stands out above all others and that's their use of the word "moderate."

In their menu, they describe the chef's salad thusly: "A moderate serving of lettuce, tomatoes, cucumbers, green and black olives, pepperoncini, onions, artichoke hearts, and green peppers, intended for one to two adults to compliment pizza or Oven Grinders. Served with sour cream garlic, sweet and sour poppy seed, and Italian dressings."

You could feed an Amish family of ten with that salad. You could plant a flag in the top and claim it for the Queen of England. You could move onto it, plant a farm, and raise corn on this salad. It should come with its own zip code.

But even then, even when confronted with this produce section on a plate, you haven't even touched the genius of the Oven Grinder's menu, for they have, in their gustatorial brilliance, created something truly ingenious and totally original: pizza pot pie.

Made from scratch out of Sicilian dough that's been raised three times to give it a delicacy and creamy crunchy perfection, and filled with whole mushrooms, whole stewed tomatoes, fist-sized chunks of Italian sausage, cheese, their homemade sauce of olive oil, garlic . . . I can't even finish this. I want to get up from my desk right now and go eat one of these things. I recall stabbing into this steaming pie and having that sauce spill out and the smell of the garlic and oil and mushrooms tumble onto the plate and the incredible, vibrant, toothsome gastroeuphoria that enveloped me in a wave of joy that started in my stomach and spread out to the far corners of the universe.

There are few dishes in Chicago that are truly original, but deep dish pizza is something we get to claim. Even there, the fight for the best is spread out over every jurisdiction, in every halfway decent Italian restaurant, their chefs bent to task over a table with a war map spread out and pepperoncinis marking their enemies ("Their dish is only an inch deep—*shallow curs!*"). The Oven Grinder is not part of this game because their deep dish pizza isn't even in a dish.

For a real challenge, may I suggest, humbly, that you attempt to finish their monumental, intimidating, and overwhelmingly delicious Italian Festa salad. I dare you. I couldn't even see over mine. My son (who only comments on video games and bodily functions) could not stop saying OH EM GEE, DAD! OH EM GEE! Which I looked up in the lexicon of eleven-year-old-boy and found stands for *Oh My God!*

Besides wedges from four ginormous tomatoes, besides the flotilla of pepperoncini, besides the battalion of whole pickled mushrooms, and not even thinking about the smoked ham, the capicola, the salami and the pepperoni—ignoring all that, forgetting all that, wrap your head around this final ingredient, nestled in among the provolone and Swiss cheese, the jewels in this verdant crown, i.e.: eight, delicious meatballs. On. A. Salad.

Genius.

The St. Valentine's Day Massacre

Everyone interested in crime who visits Chicago wants to see two things: the Biograph where Dillinger was gunned down, and the site of the St. Valentine's Day Massacre. You can still stand in front of the Biograph Theatre but the SMC Cartage Co. garage where Al Capone hired a bunch of guys to kill his Irish enemy, Bugs Moran, is a parking lot for a nursing home.

In case you've never heard about it or you're maybe obsessed with organized crime stories, here it is in bullet form:

- Al Capone is the king of the South Side Italian outfit during Prohibition. He's in a war with George "Bugs" Moran, king of the North Side Irish mob.
- The war has taken a toll on both sides, but Capone is most upset about the murders of Patsy Lolordo and Tony "The Scourge" Lombardo. He's pretty pissed about an attempt to kill his partner, Jack McGurn. So he decides to take out Moran.
- Capone's crew mocks up two fake detective cars, hires some outside guns and a couple of outside lookouts, and waits for the North Side boys to arrive.
- On the morning of Feb. 14, 1929, seven men from the North Side Irish, including an unlucky mechanic, John May, and a very unlucky mob groupie, Reinhart Schwimmer, arrived at the SMC Cartage Company at 2212 North Clark in their very best suits (not the mechanic, he was wearing overalls). Moran was either late or figured it out because he was not there.
- When the lookout saw Albert Weinshank nearing the building, he thought it was Bugs Moran (apparently, Weinshank looked like Moran). He gave the signal and the Capone crew entered the building and nabbed the North Side Irish.
- The men were lined up against the wall and gunned down. They were shot by two men using Thompson machine guns who fired seventy bullets and two shotgun blasts from two fake cops.

Keep in mind that this was 1929. No cell phones, no video cameras, no Motorola headsets. They had to use hand signals and lookouts, and they were freaks about face recognition. Capone knew that the North Side gang would make anybody from the South Side Italians just sitting around "reading a newspaper" so he outsourced his lookouts and put them in position to see a block on either side of the garage. One of them, according to local lore, sat in an upstairs room of the little Victorian brownstone that now houses Chicago Pizza and Oven Grinder and gave the leader the signal that sent the fake cops in the back door and the real killers in the front.

You can have a slice and a calzone under the same roof where the world's most notorious whack was ordered.

Capone was less than thrilled by the killing, since he missed Moran and only made the war worse. The two tommy gunners marched out of the building in front of the two fake cops so everyone watching thought it was under control. Later, they thought the cops were in on the killing.

The violent cruelty and gruesome body count of the crime changed public opinion about the mob and finally got the attention of the feds. Two years later, Capone was arrested for tax evasion.

Branko's Submarines

1118 W. Fullerton Ave.

773-472-4873

Cuisine: *hot dogs, beef*

Hot dogs like your mom used to make if your mom ever made hot dogs. Mine didn't and therein may lie the impetus, the original inspiration for both my passions of police work and eating at cheap cafés: not making your kid hot dogs is criminal. I'm lucky I didn't end up in prison.

This Fullerton Avenue eatery is across the street from DePaul University. Although the menu is standard hot dog joint, it's the service that makes this place special. It really does seem like your mom is serving you lunch. The lady behind the counter has been serving college students for so long she treats everybody like they're a teenager. If you want to feel like you're in college again, go to Branko's and have a hot dog or a Polish dragged through the garden.*

Nearby DePaul University provides Branko's with most of their customers, so expect it to be crowded with collegiates. However, quick service keeps the line moving and the friendliness of the staff makes it bearable. Even when there is a line, you can get your food and eat it in the span of a normal lunch half-hour. The prices are comparable to other fast food places in the area, which means that you can get a decent meal for under ten bucks.

Caribbean American Baking Co.

1539 W. Howard St.
773-761-0700
www.caribbeanamericanbakery.com
Cuisine: *baked goods, Carribean pizza puffs*

It may seem strange to include a bakery in a book like this. However, the Carribean bakery is unusual. In addition to the sweet baked goods, like danishes, coconut macaroons, banana cake, and the incredible coconut drops, this bakery serves hot food: jerk chicken patties, beef patties, and spicy callaloo patties. The Carribean bakery doesn't have tables; everything you buy is to go. It doesn't have any décor to speak of, but in this case it's because they so put much effort into the food.

---

*"Dragged through the garden" means getting a hot dog with everything on it. Purists say that you should only put mustard, onions, and neon green relish on a hot dog. Most Chicago hot dog joints put tomatoes, pickles, lettuce, and celery salt on it. To get all the veggies heaped on your dog, tell the person behind the counter to "drag it through the garden"!

StreetWise

In 1979, I was a young police officer in 018. Once, we stopped at a restaurant on North Lincoln Park West. Inside there was one table with about six diners who were rather intoxicated and raucous, but not yet police-worthy. Once they saw the big city police they seemed to quiet down. The restaurant manager came by our table and thanked us for coming in. He knew our presence had calmed the wild throng . . .

After we ate and were preparing to leave, two of the noisy guys headed over to our table and picked up our check. It was none other than John Belushi and Dan Akroyd. They had just gotten into town to film *The Blues Brothers*. We ended up giving them a ride back to their hotel and it began a summer-long friendship that included regular access to their private club, (a shuttered bar formerly known as the Sneak Joint, located across the street from The Second City).

Akroyd was a big police fan and always a wonderful and respectful host, learning our first names even amongst a hoard of fans. He never asked nor expected anything in return. When the cast was done filming, they came back months later to begin a national concert tour with the Blues Band. They never forgot us, and we ended up with backstage passes to their concert at what was then Poplar Creek . . . and it all started with lunch! Oh, the memories!"   *—Sgt. Kent Erickson, Ret.*

A Jamaican pizza puff (or meat patty as they call it) costs about two bucks. You're talking about spicy ground beef in a delicious, flaky shell, deep fried in (do not ask). There is a constant demand for these delicious pastries and meat pies, and I've never been there and seen them run out. They must make and sell a ton of them, because they always have some freshly made.

Like all great cafés, this one does a lot of catering. You can get pans full of jerk pork, curry goat, brown-stew chicken, and oxtail for parties.

StreetWise

One of the "workin' girls" on Madison wanted to get out of the way for the night. One of the regulars, too smart to be out in the world like she was, but who were we to judge?

Wind chill of about -60˚F; she walked up and tapped on the passenger window of our pea-soup green '86 Caprice. She made a little loot and she didn't want ol' boy kicking a pocket in her ass and taking it from her.

"Ya ain't got nothin' on ya right?"

"No officer, I know better than that."

"OK, just turn around and stick ya hands in the window thumbs up." *click-click* (handcuffs)

"Ya hungry?"

"Yes!"

"Hey pardner, let's roll over to Jim's on Maxwell and Halsted and get her somethin' to eat."

She ate and was in a warm place. She also filled out the arrest report for us except for the charge for soliciting rides (very good penmanship). She also gave us some good info that led to some pretty nice arrests a few days later. The W/C gave the OK and we took her to Women's Central at 1121. She said "thank you" as the detention aide escorted her in.

Nothing spectacular. No chase, no car wrecks, no gun battles. Just a memory of how the odd coincidence of policing, cheap eats, and treating people right led to actionable info and decent arrests. —*Anonymous Officer*

Clark Street Dog

3040 N. Clark St.

773-281-6690

www.clarkstdog.com

Cuisine: *hot dogs, late-night*

When you're working midnights, eating is tough. You find yourself on a schedule that's opposite everyone else. You find yourself eating scrambled eggs at 4:00 in the afternoon and craving hot dogs at 3:00 a.m. I realize this also happens after you've been drinking all night, but this book is about where *cops* eat, not where *drunks* eat.

Clark Street is located at the intersection of Clark, Halsted, and Barry. The three converging streets make up a triangular piece of property where the restaurant sits. On one side is a coffee shop, on another, a liquor store. It's also bracketed by a Walgreens and a CVS pharmacy. Add to that the fact that it is only a block south of Belmont and Clark, a hub of the GLBT community, and a block north of Illinois Masonic Hospital, a hub of the victims of violent crime and psychological disorder community, and you get an interesting show playing out in front of you when you stop for a dog.

The food is good, especially the Polish sausage. I've had the beef too, which is as good as any on Taylor Street. The prices are on the high side of this book, a lunch costs close to $10, but the show makes it worth it.

Just recently, on Barry, within sight of Clark Street Dogs, a fire broke out in an apartment building. What happened, we found out later, was that some young guys were partying, passed out, and left a candle burning. For some reason, this was a call that built slowly. It was the middle of a slow morning; Officer Megan Hart was stopped by a citizen and told about the fire. She radioed the possibility of a fire, but didn't see any smoke.

Now the scary part. As Megan went to check it out, the dispatcher assigned someone to help her. Everyone was pretty far away. That happens sometimes, but everyone was either down on a job, or at opposite ends of the district from Clark and Halsted. That area has some of the worst traffic and there is no way anyone is getting there fast without lighting up the lights and siren.

Megan hadn't seen any smoke though. Other coppers started to head that way, but everybody (those who were paying attention, anyway) thought that it was all bullshit. It's a high density area after all, and there are usually several calls whenever even the most minor fire starts. A few minutes later, Megan's back on the air, yelling that it's bona fide, and that she was evacuating the building, and where the hell was everybody?!?

That got everybody rushing in, sirens screaming, lights flashing. Traffic was blocked off. The fire department put the fire out, which was small, but caused a lot of smoke. There were lots of fire trucks, which are fun to watch; traffic got all locked up, and the best view was from the front windows of Clark Street Dog.

Officer Megan Hart was awarded the Lifesaving Award for what she did. She ran into the burning building alone and got quite a few people out, some of whom she had to wake up. One person succumbed to the smoke and died. This shows how dangerous the situation was. Megan did a great job.

StreetWise

The most popular watering hole in the late sixties, where just about all the police brass could be found, especially through the late evening hours was known as "Little Jack's" on West Madison Street.

The food was good and the service not far behind. It was usually about the time your order was being served the street operator would call to give you an assignment in your area. The majority of your order would be left behind while you and your partner headed for the door, but not without squaring things with the cashier. If that timely interruption didn't take place, the then supervising captain, affectionately known as "Jungle Jim," would make his rounds in the hope of catching someone with an unfastened button on their blouse to write up to meet his evening quota.   **—Robert Hulsman, Ret**

Cy's Crab House

3819 N. Ashland Ave.
773-883-8900
www.cyscrab.com
Cuisine: *seafood*

Cy's holds a special place in my heart: when I was a teenage beat
cop, this is where my family went to celebrate. It's not one of the
cheapest places you can go for a quick bite, but the food's East
Coast fresh and they usually get it to the table pretty fast.

Cy's is a sit-down place, and that makes it tough for police
officers to eat there. But it's a great place to take the wife
on date night. The location is in a gentrified residential
neighborhood, about five blocks from Wrigley Field, and there
are several nice bars in the area, so it's also a very nice place to
take a walk after dinner.

Known for their seafood, Cy's also sports a fine Mediterranean
section that includes shish kabobs. But it's fish, it's crabs, it's
lobster that's their mother's milk. I love the grilled Lake Superior
whitefish. (I've tried doing it myself at home, and can't even come
close.) I think it's because their fish is so fresh. My wife, Anne,
loves the grilled shrimp and scallops with linguini.

No one's going to Cy's for fast food. They're going for a longer
and more expensive sit-down dinner. However, it qualifies for this
book for two reasons:

1) Soup. Cy's makes phenomenal soup. Their clam chowder's
so thick you can hold the spoon upside down without spilling
the soup on your uniform pants. (Somehow I still get some on my
tie.) However, it's the lobster bisque that makes it worth the risk
of punching in a few minutes late. Real chunks of lobster and just
a little spicy. Man, it's good.

2) Shrimp and oysters for sixty cents and wings for thirty-five
cents apiece at the bar. Police officers do not sit at the bar to eat.
I don't know if it's forbidden but I bet that the first time some

poor cop sat at the bar to eat, a *Sun-Times* reporter snapped a picture of him for the next day's front page and his life would then be hell. The point is that the oyster special is at the bar, and while they might be nice and let the police eat oysters for sixty cents at a table, they also may not let you.

Duke of Perth

2913 N. Clark St.

773-477-1741

www.dukeofperth.com

Cuisine: *fish fry, seventy-five kinds of Scotch*

You know what is missing in our modern high-speed world? A good old-fashioned fish fry. Every Wednesday and Friday you can eat your fill at this Scottish pub in Lincoln Park. This is actually a terrible place to go while you're working. Not because the food is bad—people from the United Kingdom know their food is generally terrible; I wouldn't feed it to a guy in jail. But fish they can do. No, the problem isn't the food, the problem is temptation. To sit there in uniform and look at seventy-five different bottles of Scotch and say "I'll just have water." Could there be anything worse?

I've always believed in what Churchill said: "Good Scotch is God's reward for a hard day's work." The Duke of Perth is a place better saved as a reward.

In addition to their twice weekly fish fries, The Duke of Perth boasts a selection of good Scottish dishes like shepherd's pie and great burgers with cool names like the "Robert the Bruce Burger." I don't know who Robert or Bruce is, but they must have done something great to have this burger named after them.

Of course I'm kidding. Just like everyone else, I know that Robert the Bruce led the Scottish army in their successful quest to secure independence from England in 1374. I mean really, who doesn't know that? Still, I don't think that the guy who eventually rose to be King of Scotland could ever count among his many accomplishments anything even approaching the magnitude of this cheeseburger. If Robert the Bruce were alive today, he'd be begging someone to let him out of that tomb. Once he got out, he'd beg to go to the Duke of Perth.

Eat a Pita
3155 N. Halsted St.
773-929-6727
www.eatapitachicago.com
Cuisine: *pita, stir-fry*

This book is spilling over with food that's fast and tasty which usually means battered and fried. But not at Eat a Pita. Eat a Pita is great for those days when you realize that you really have to start eating better.

Eat a Pita serves healthy fast food. Their soup is made fresh daily, and is very good. I don't think soup is discussed enough in this book, but I think it's very important. When you work outside in the winter, nothing is better than a bowl of soup. Sure, a cup of coffee is nice, but after six or seven, you can't really aim straight anymore. Plus, you're hungry.

If your good intentions to eat healthy weaken by the time you get to the counter, they also serve fully loaded baked potatoes and burgers.

The restaurant is always clean and well lit when I visit, and the people who work there are very nice and friendly. The prices aren't bad, so you can't use cost as an excuse to go to McDonald's.

Eat a Pita has two locations in Chicago: the one listed here and one on Division Street, near Rush.

Glenn's Diner

1820 W. Montrose Ave.

773-506-1720

www.glennsdiner.com

Cuisine: *seafood, American, cereal*

Glenn's has an interesting recent history. Last winter the street in front of it collapsed. In the middle of the night, but before the bar across the way closed, the street decided to become a very large hole.

Some of the people in the bar were still shaking the next morning when they described what happened: They were drinking, it was a cold, clear night. One guy was looking out into the street when the curbside tree fell down. By the time he realized how weird that was, everybody else was running toward the back door, sure that the building was going to fall down next. A water main had broken, and the street eventually sank about ten feet. The brink of the sinkhole came all the way up to the buildings, but nobody fell in, and nobody was hurt.

Over the next week, the street was rebuilt in a stunning display of engineering and teamwork. I mention it here because no one else has, and we will probably never see its like again.

Glenn's was one of the buildings that survived. And thankfully so. The café serves great seafood, and some unusual seafood. I've seen shark on the chalkboard menus, although I didn't try it myself. They also have steaks and a little pasta. When I went there for lunch, the service was great. Even the owner came out to say hello.

Try the fish po'boy. This sandwich was incredible. The roll it was served on was crusty and warm; it gave the impression that it was baked fresh in the kitchen just before they made the sandwich. The fish was perfectly done and had a firmness and texture that seems to be lacking a lot when you order fish. I had it with some fresh fruit that was juicy and cold and was a perfect counterpoint to the sandwich.

I have one criticism. They had clam chowder by the cup or the bowl. I am a clam chowder nut, and I decided to get a cup. I thought the price was a little high ($3.50) but figured that when they said "cup" they really meant "small bowl" like they do in so many other places. I was wrong. The soup was great, but they brought it out in a cup, a fairly small cup at that. So just be prepared. The soup is good, but the portions are small.

Also, there's a wall of cereal boxes. When I asked why, I was told that they serve whatever cereal was there. They said that it was a big seller. So for anything from seafood to cereal, try Glenn's.

Gulliver's

2727 W. Howard St.
773-338-2166
www.gulliverspizza.com
Cuisine: *pizza*

Gulliver's is another iconic neighborhood place. Up at the northernmost edge of the city, in a place you don't expect to find really good restaurants, is Gulliver's. It's a surprise only to those who don't come from the neighborhood. Gulliver's has a full bar, and the prices are very good for a restaurant with this kind of quality food. You could get a steak by yourself or a pizza if you have the family with you. Generations of neighborhood residents have celebrated their birthdays, graduations, and first communions there. The service is fast, and you can get lunch in enough time to get back on the beat before the inspector finds you.

The most memorable thing about Gulliver's is the décor. The owner collects antiques, and the restaurant is full of them. From Tiffany lamps to tables that would hold all of King Arthur's knights, Gulliver's feels like a visit to a museum, only with really good food. The antiques are mostly from between 1860 to 1915; what the menu calls the Victorian and Art Nouveau Era.

Recently, we heard that the restaurant had new owners, so we went and talked to George Varvitsiotis, the new guy. The menu and the décor have not changed and he says that the menu will not change anytime soon. The only addition is an outdoor patio dining area as lavishly decorated as the inside of the restaurant. Rumors have it that the pizza recipe changed with the new owners and a lot of the priceless antiques were sold off. These are baseless lies and scandalous imprecations. Varvitsiotis bought the recipe with the building. The lamps, naked alabaster women, and the giant bottle of Scotch are all still there. Each is tagged with a six-digit number AS IF THEY ARE FOR SALE, but, my sources swear to me, they've always been tagged.

When I was a teenager, I ate mostly pizza at Gulliver's, and the pizza is good. However, they have a huge menu, and a lot of it is very good. If you are trying to eat healthy, you should have the chicken walnut salad. During one of my frequent try-to-lose-weight phases I ordered that and it was the first time I ever had orange slices on a salad. The calamari is good too. Not too many tentacles. If you have the time, or if you ordered the salad and are feeling particularly proud that you stuck to your diet, try the

Bacon Candy

When Dave told me we had to include a recipe in this book, I was stumped. The theme is cheap eats and the idea is that these are the go-to places for Dave and other beat cops who don't have the time to sit down and eat and don't want to blow a wad of cash only to be interrupted in the middle of lunch to go fight crime. So what do you cook for these guys? It has to be portable, delicious, and cheap. Preparation time is important but not critical. Gumbo is out because you don't pack soup. Deviled eggs are out because how the hell do you carry them? There is only one solution, a food so delicious, so ridiculously divine, snacktacular, and above all totally weird. I'm talking about candied bacon.

I know, it sounds like something you'd get in Chinatown (actually, you're more likely to get candied squid in Chinatown, and no, I'm not making that up) but trust me. This is one of my favorite party tricks and comes to me from one of my antique Amish cookbooks. This is old-school finger food so fire up a defibrillator and put your apron on.

Mr. Garlington's Famous Bacon Candy

First, get a whole lot of bacon. Cheap, skinny bacon you can read through. This recipe does not require the hand-crafted, independently farmed, organic free-range massaged and cuddled pork you might buy at Whole Foods. Get the generic stuff.

Put the bacon on a rack over a pan in the oven and bake it till it's just almost crispy. 350 degrees for about ten minutes. Take it out to cool and leave the oven on. Drain the fat off the pan.

While it's baking, mix up the following:

1 tablespoon Dijon mustard
½ cup brown sugar lightly packed
2 tablespoons red wine
a dash—A FREAKING DASH; NOT A SPOONFUL, JUST A DASH! A DASH! A PINCH! A SMIDGEN! of cayenne pepper.

Now coat the bacon with the sauce and put it in the pan on a wire rack. Use all the sauce! Bake the bacon until the sauce begins to bubble and then remove it, laying it on wax paper until it cools. IT SHOULD BE DRY TO THE TOUCH—NOT STICKY. If it's sticky, bake it a few more minutes. It took me a while to get this last part right but you have to have confidence here and leave the bacon in the oven slightly longer than your instinct tells you to. When you see it bubbling, you're going to want to yank it out. DON'T. Count to ten. Wait. Have courage. Then yank it.

Once the bacon is cool, cut the strips into pieces and put them all into Tupperware. Beware, these things are even more addicting than deviled eggs mud pie sundae. It's fantastic, and everyone deserves a sweet treat sometimes.

John Barleycorn

3524 N. Clark St.

773-549-6000

www.johnbarleycorn.com

Cuisine: *chicken wings, clam chowder*

John Barleycorn is just down the street from Wrigley Field. It's a great place to go after a ball game for a beer. It's a loud place and seems noisy all the time, even if there are only a few people there. I think it has something to do with the acoustics, I don't know. The noise is great after a Cubs win but seems a little incongruous after a loss. Of course, anything but abject silence seems a little incongruous after a Cubs loss.

Barleycorn prides themselves on their wings and clam chowder. Both are very good. If you like your chicken wings crispy, then you'll love them here. They have a chipotle BBQ sauce that has just a little kick and a lot of tang.

The clam chowder is very good. It has more actual clams than anywhere else I've gone. It's only available in the fall and winter, however, so you won't get it until after the Cubs are done playing. Or until they are in the World Series (maybe next year).

[Dave, are you nuts? The Cubs are never going to win a World Series, ever. They can't. Not because they're bad ballplayers (they are) but because of Cub love, the nut of the obsession, is losing. Winning the World Series would be like finding Bigfoot riding the Loch Ness monster into Atlantis. It would kill the mystery. *The Cubs have to lose. They have to continue to lose.* They have to swerve dangerously close to winning; they have to get into the pennant series; they have to get our hopes up. Then they have to fail—and fail miserably. They have to scourge our bright hopes across the sharp rocks of uselessness, year after year, because that's what keeps filling the seats in Wrigley when every other ball club in America looks like a Wal-Mart parking lot on Christmas. We don't love the Cubs because they win. We love the cubs because they *almost* win. The day Barleycorn or any other renowned Chicago pub has a World Series celebration you can bet your badge I'll be there—doing shots with Jimmy Hoffa and D.B. Cooper.—C.G.]

The rest of the small menu is solid sandwiches and pub food. Their calamari is very good, and on Wednesdays they have all-you-can-eat fish and chips.

If you are going to Barleycorn, you're going for the atmosphere, not the food; more than a dozen TVs with all kinds of sports on them, loud music overhead, and a very nice staff. The pub is beautiful. It has extremely high ceilings, great woodwork throughout, and seems very comfortable for a place that size.

Barleycorn has a party room/meeting room upstairs that has been used for a lot of fundraising and promotion parties. When it gets extremely busy downstairs, they open the upstairs bar. During the baseball season, Clark Street is probably the safest place in the city. There are tons of police around all the time. During the summer, even when the Cubs are out of town, all of the restaurants and bars, including Barleycorn, open their front windows. The cacophony of sounds and smells is a pleasant assault on your senses, while the cool breezes off the lake feel wonderful.

Crabby Kim's
3655 N. Western Ave.
773-404-8756
Cuisine: *cheeseburgers, bikinis*

(Co-author's note: It has come to my attention that, due to environmental circumstances, Sgt. Haynes's opinion of Crabby Kim's may be less than objective. Proceed with caution.)

Attention all you midnight cops: This is the only place I know where you can get off work at 7:00 a.m. and get an omelet and a beer served by a woman in a bikini. I realize that most men have a wife at home that is more than willing to throw on a bikini and bring beer and cheeseburgers to them while they're watching the big game on a fifty-inch plasma TV. For those who don't fit into the norm, Crabby Kim's is the place to go.

The food is first rate. I think the cheeseburgers are the best. Cooked any way you want them, served with fries, and all the condiments in recycled six-pack holders. Kim's also has a large selection of other sandwiches and even salads.

All the bartenders wear bikinis all year round and they are very nice and professional. The cooking is done by a guy behind the grill, so you won't be able to see what happens when a woman in a bikini fries bacon.

The food is all below ten bucks, and the drinks are comparable to the rest of the bars in the neighborhood, so it's a pretty good deal.

Misericordia Greenhouse Inn

6300 N. Ridge Ave.
773-273-4182
www.misericordia.com/shops/greenhouse_inn.aspx
Cuisine: *bakery, soups, sandwiches*

Most Chicagoans know of Misericordia from their April "Candy Days" fundraiser. You've given them loose change and they've given you a piece of candy. What you probably don't know is they also have a really good restaurant.

For decades the Fannie May caramel pop was the signature candy, until the forces of corporate change ended the Fannie May company. Now, Misericordia gives away Jelly Bellies.

My wife, sister-in-law, and mother-in-law have all worked or volunteered at Misericordia and we occasionally had lunch at

the Greenhouse Inn, a restaurant on the grounds of the home. The Greenhouse Inn restaurant and bakery raises money for the cause—but it also gives the residents a real job and creates a positive community. Sister Rosemary Connelly started Misericordia home in 1969 because she felt that the community of developmentally disabled people was woefully underserved. Sister Connelly believed these disabled adults could hold down jobs and function as a community. She was right, and the entire Misericordia campus stands as a monument to her vision.

The food in the Greenhouse Inn is as good as any other restaurant. In my view the salad bar is the best deal. There are always two types of homemade soup that are part of the package, or can be ordered by themselves. You can also order á la carte. Cards and pencils are provided and the customer is expected to mark off each choice on their menu card so there are no mistakes. The menu has daily specials and sandwiches. They even have peanut butter and jelly for the kids.

After lunch, check out their "Hearts and Flour" bakery. They have fantastic baked goods, and the best inside-out cookies I've ever had. Inside-out cookies are chocolate cookies with white chocolate chips. Most of the employees are residents of Misericordia and are supervised by professionals.

It's actually an uplifting experience; when you go there you may have all of your normal problems on your mind, and then, after you are around the residents awhile, you realize how happy they are when they have monumentally more difficult problems then you. When I go to Misericordia, I always leave in a good mood. As I write this, I realize I don't go there enough.

Miska's Bar

2156 W. Belmont Ave.

773-935-5373

Cuisine: *soups, sandwiches*

Miska's is a liquor store. Right away that should get your attention. When I got a new boss, just to mess around, I said that I was going to the liquor store to get lunch. She wasn't amused.

Miska's is not your average liquor store, however. And when I say that I'm talking about this particular store. I know that there is a chain of Miska's and we have purposely left non-local chains out of this book so that we can cover local eateries. I've been in other Miska's liquor stores, and none of them have a deli, so I'm assuming that this one is unique.

They serve homemade soup and deli sandwiches made by Polish ladies who apparently think I'm too thin. They really pile on the meat, and the soup is usually very good. When I say usually, I mean every time I've tasted it, but I would have to be near starvation to eat cabbage soup, and they seem to serve that a lot.

The store is laid out so that you have to get your sandwich and then walk through the liquor aisles to get to the cash register, which prompts some strange looks when you're in a police uniform.

The sandwiches are right around five bucks, and the soup is two. If you're not on duty, they have a bar in the rear to sit and drink away the afternoon. Other than that, they don't have very much in the way of seating.

Moe's Cantina

3518 N. Clark St.
773-248-0002
www.moescantina.com
Cuisine: *Mexican*

Moe's is a new Wrigleyville icon-in-the-making. Mostly designed
to accommodate the after-Cubs game crowd, the food is
surprisingly good. The prices are standard Wrigleyville, which is
to say, high. The food is served tapas style, so you'll want to order
a couple of entrées for each person.

The lamb chops are great. They come four to the order. They
also make a very good salsa and chips. The salsa is homemade
with a fruity taste and a little fire. I didn't think that combo
would work, but a friend ordered it, so I tried it. Thumbs up!

Moe's has huge garage doors that make up the front wall,
and in the summer they open them up, which makes for a great
Chicago setting. The restaurant itself is very comfortable. Loud
enough to be fun, but the acoustics work out so that you can
carry on a conversation easily.

Moody's Pub

5910 N. Broadway
773-275-2696
www.moodyspub.com
Cuisine: *burgers, pub grub*

Moody's Pub is dark and woody. It's a neighborhood bar and grill
with a great patio. You can come and have one of their legendary
cheeseburgers near one of three waterfalls. Trees growing on
the deck provide shade during the day and give a beautiful
atmosphere on a summer or fall evening. Inside, each wooden
table has a bowl of peanuts, and the fires are lit during the winter

giving it an Olde English vibe.

They have both winter and summer menus. During the summer, some of the heavier stuff comes off—food like steaks and chops—and they serve mostly sandwiches. They have salads and a shrimp basket as well.

One of their best sandwiches, both summer and winter, is the Sloppy Joe. This is not your high-school cafeteria Sloppy Joe, but an adult version: huge, messy, and delicious. You practically have to eat it with a spoon. My favorite is the Moody Bleu Burger, the rock-and-roll pun aside. It's big, it's juicy, and it's got bleu cheese on it—what more could you ask for?

Moody's is known for its onion rings. They're homemade, not frozen. The onion rings are so good that they run out often enough that they had to put on the menu that you can order them "when available."

Across the street from Moody's is the Broadway Armory. If you have time, check it out. The Broadway Armory was originally designed as a giant ice rink, but was used as an armory from World War I until after World War II. The Chicago Park District began using it as an indoor park in 1979. It's our largest, and as far as I know, only completely indoor park.

As I was writing this, I was trying to think of the last time I was in the armory as part of my job. Back on December 31, 1999, people believed that all of the technology was going to fail because of a computer glitch. The Chicago Police Department cancelled all time off. I had a briefing in the Broadway Armory that night, and then went out on patrol, expected to quell the riots that were sure to follow the technological blackout. No blackout, no riots, nothing. It's hard to believe that it's been ten years since then. Imagine what we are doing now that we will look back on in ten years and ask, "How could we be that stupid?"

Smoke Shack

800 W. Altgeld St.

773-248-8886

Cuisine: *barbeque*

The Smoke Shack is a brand new barbecue place at Altgeld and Halsted. They have a nice open décor and picnic table seating. The seating encourages strangers to share tables and conversation. Ribs are served St. Louis style, which is a dry rub, or with sauce. Dry rub is a dry mixture of spices rubbed into the ribs before they're cooked. I've tried making ribs with both sauces and rubs. If you have a good rub, I think ribs can actually be better. It's a matter of taste, however. You should try ribs both ways to determine your own preference.

A full slab of ribs with all the trimmings is just over $20, which isn't unusual for ribs in Chicago, but it's pretty expensive for lunch on a cop's salary. However, they also have a terrific pulled pork sandwich for around $6. They have hamburgers and hot dogs that are even less expensive.

With any BBQ joint, you have to talk about the sauce, and in this case it's very tangy with a hint of spice. You really feel it in the back of your jaw when you take the first bite. The homemade coleslaw is colorful. French fries are served in a wire cone, which as far as I can tell serves no purpose other than to look good. Utensils are not given with the meal. You have to go up to the counter and get them for yourself. That's important to know if, like me, you are lazy. Nothing's worse than getting your food, smelling it, then sitting down and realizing you have to get up again for a fork. That six feet to the counter looks like a mile.

Smoke Shack is one block east of the Biograph Theatre, where John Dillinger was betrayed by the woman in red and killed by Christian Bale.

Spacca Napoli

1769 W. Sunnyside Ave.

773-878-2420

spaccanapolipizzeria.com

Cuisine: *Neapolitan pizza*

The first time I was in Spacca Napoli, I was called there on a Monday night by one of my officers who was investigating a possible burglary. A customer had come to have dinner, and when she walked into the restaurant, she realized that no one was there. No customers, no workers, nobody. Fearing a burglary, she called the police. When we got there, our keen investigative abilities told us that the door had probably been left open by a worker. While we were waiting to see if the desk could get in touch with the owner, Jonathan Goldsmith, he walked in. He had gone to volunteer at a soup kitchen and forgot to lock the door when he left.

I got to talking to Jonathan and realized that something was wrong. Nobody should be allowed to be that happy in his work.

Go have some pizza at Spacca Napoli and get him talking about all the history and intricacies that go into making Neapolitan-style pizza. It's fascinating. It's also humbling to meet someone who has really found his niche in life and is happy with it. Anybody who goes on vacation to Sicily to find the perfect buffalo's milk cheese to put on pizza is dedicated. And he sure makes a good pie too.

Neapolitan pizza is different from the normal pizza in Chicago. It's more like New York pizza, with a thin, soft crust. It's cooked in a wood-fired oven and only takes about ten minutes to make. The flavors, spices, and toppings are much more subtle. Here was my first taste of pizza margherita, which has sauce, cheese, and fresh basil arranged to honor the Italian flag and, according to the History Channel, is the pie that put pizza on the map.

Spacca Napoli offers an outside patio only a few blocks from former governor Rod Blagojevich's home, so you might just see him and his family stopping by for pizza. Or jogging by. Or filming a reality show. Or selling custom license plates.

I never had a personal interaction with Blago, but he once had an office that was just a few doors away from the restaurant. During the famous investigation, the feds set up surveillance, including a camera, on the railroad tracks across the street. I know that the camera was used for the purposes of finding out who came and went at the office, but they could probably see who ate at the restaurant, too. Anybody who ate there during that time is possibly part of the investigation.

Vienna Beef Café

2501 N. Damen Ave.
773-435-2277
www.viennabeef.com/cafemenu
Cuisine: *hot dogs*

Vienna hot dogs have long claimed the title of Chicago's hot dog. The famous poster they use to advertise is a classic, with a giant hot dog on top of Navy Pier with boats and a helicopter putting the fixings on. It captures things we treasure about Chicago: the lake, the skyline, and a freakish, hallucinatory devotion to hot dogs.

The Vienna factory has a store that sells their gear. One of the big city benefits of Chicago is that we make a lot of stuff here. If you go to the place where they make stuff, you can usually get that stuff cheaper. Also, you can get seconds. Seconds are what factories sell when there is some imperfection in their product. It's still good, but doesn't look good enough to sell. My mom always used to go to the Fannie May factory when I was a kid because they would sell the Mint Meltaways that weren't perfectly square at a discount. The same goes for Vienna. You can get really good deals on hot dogs from their factory store.

Oh yeah, you can eat there too. They serve hot dogs.
Helicopters not included.

Wiener Circle

2622 N. Clark St.

773-477-7444

www.wienercircle.net

Cuisine: *hot dogs, cheeseburgers*

The only place to get really good greasy food in Lincoln Park
after 2:00 a.m. Need I say more? Well probably, but that just
about says it all. The Weiner Circle is on Clark street, south of
Wrigleyville, and in the middle of the night it's packed with
people trying to get food in their stomachs so they can sober up
to drive home.

That doesn't work, by the way. If you drink too much, leave your
car and take a cab. In Chicago, you will get no breaks for drunk
driving, and only time can sober you up—not coffee or food.

Whether you are drinking or not, though, the food at Wiener
Circle is great. Classic Chicago hot dogs and cheddar burgers
cooked over an open flame for a few bucks.

A caveat for our esteemed visitors and people taking their
children out for hot dogs at two in the morning: There's a
prevailing trend at this café for drunken customers to yell their
order in the most profane, flagitious, puerile, nun-offending
jargon they can muster, then cap their order with an invective
meant to cast aspersions on the nature of the order taker's sex,
lineage, or alarming sexual proclivity. Please don't call the cops
about this. We already know. It's a cultural thing. It's part of
Chicago. You pay good money for the prime-time version over at
Ed Debevic's. This is the real version. Just roll with it and join in.
I promise you probably won't get arrested. Check YouTube clips
in advance for some hints.

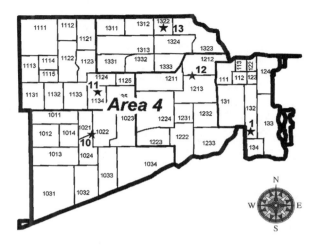

"Ask not what you can do for your country.
Ask what's for lunch."
—*Orson Welles*

StreetWise

In 1997 I worked in 011 on first watch with my partner and best friend Jeff. At the end of the evening, (0100 hours) Homerun Inn Pizza on 31st and Kostner would call the various district stations and have a car come pick up several pizzas to be distributed among the watch. Jeff and I were asked—only once—to go pick up the pizzas by the watch secretary and this is why:

Jeff and I picked up seven extra-large pizzas of various types. We happened to find the sausage, which just happened to fit perfectly on the dashboard of the old bubble Chevy Caprice. In the slow fifteen-minute drive back to 011 we were able to eat the entire extra-large sausage pizza. We would have gotten away with it, but I walked in to the watch commander's office and put down the other pizzas, exposing the red pizza sauce stain on my blue vest cover, which I hadn't noticed. The district secretary counted the pizzas, now six, and chased us out of 011! We were not selfish, just hungry.

—Det. John Campbell, Unit 630

Finkel's Deli

926 N. Branch St.
312-829-1699
Cuisine: *deli*

Finkel's is located next to Kendall College (see p. 81), so when you pull into the parking lot and walk towards the door, you have a choice to make: gourmet food cooked by students who may or may not know what they are doing, or deli sandwiches made by people who *really* know what they are doing.

I've never been to New York (and never will go there unless I'm dragged kicking and screaming) so I don't know how Finkel's compares to those old-time delis, but I know great sandwiches and these are the kind of mouthwatering, eye-rolling, stomach-blessing nuclear bombs of gastronomic euphoria. The corned beef is in the top two I've ever tasted. (See Manny's, p. 82 for the other one).

The service is a little slow, but they serve a lot of people at lunch, and the food is worth the wait. The décor is basic deli, with red-checked tablecloths and a counter. You don't have to go to the counter to order, but it adds to the experience. What's really too bad is the view, though that's no fault of the owners. The deli is situated immediately adjacent to the Chicago River, but the gravel parking lot and the huge factory across the river make for terrible scenery.

I used to teach the Chicago police antiterrorism course at nearby Near North School. We went to Finkel's every week. Finkel's is very popular with people who work in the area, and that means a very nice mix of white collar, blue collar, and police.

They have great soup.

Foodlife Water Tower

835 N. Michigan Ave.
312-355-3663
www.foodlifechicago.com
Cuisine: *various*

In Chicago, the police can sometimes work in their off-duty hours for the Chicago Transit Authority. The officers spend eight hours on one street in the city and follow buses and catch rides on the same buses in an effort to reduce crime. It's pretty boring, but the perk is extra money, and you get to see parts of the city you don't normally see. When I used to do this, I got the

Michigan Avenue route a few times and discovered the Water Tower food court, Foodlife.

Look, I know this place isn't exactly blue collar and I know it's not exactly cheap. It's not much different from any strip mall food court in any midwestern town except it has more people with purse dogs. You don't pay at the individual places. When you walk into the food court, you're given a plastic card, like a credit card. As you get food from the individual stands, they swipe your card.

Thus, you might get soup and appetizers from one restaurant, drinks from another, and your entrée from yet another. However, you only pay one bill, at the end of your meal as you leave. It's a great concept, and you are willing to spend more, because you seem to be getting what you want. The prices can run high, but if you carefully watch when you order stuff, you can have a good, filling meal on the cheap.

I've never had a bad meal there. They have good soups at one station and Mexican food at another. They also have the standard hot dog fare, and the dessert stand is fantastic. They even have a health food section with organic produce and wheat germ. As far as the wheat germ category goes, I don't go there, so I just can't advise you. I'm willing to run into a burning building to save someone, or get into a gun battle to protect a child, but you have to draw the line somewhere, and I'm not drinking pureed grass, no matter how good they say it is for me.

This is also a great place to take kids. The Water Tower mall is a little highbrow, but it's right across the street from the Water Tower, the Museum of Contemporary Art, and the Hancock building—all great tourist spots. Foodlife allows you to get whatever kind of food *you* want, while letting your kids get the kind of food *they* want. It's already loud so the kids can run around and yell without bothering your fellow eaters.

StreetWise

While on a station run to pick up cases of pop and food for our once-a-week BBQ at 011 (we have a civilian lock up aide who is a trained chef—we stole him from 012), I pulled the marked squad car into the pick-up lane of a local Jewel, went in and picked up the stuff. While loading it into the trunk, I see Mr. Smooth Criminal come running out of the GNC with a full display case in his hands. He looks at me with a priceless "oh shit" look. I just started laughing. His feeble escape attempt ended shortly after. As he was cuffed and in my squad car, I had to ask him, "Hey didn't you see the POLICE car parked in front when you went into the store? All he said was "no." —*P.O. A Baumann; 011 second watch*

Jimmy's Red Hots

4000 W. Grand Ave.

773-384-9513

www.jimmysredhots.com

Cuisine: *hot dogs, tamales*

NO KETCHUP. I've said it before, and I'll say it again: ketchup is not a bad thing. The people at Jimmy's don't agree. There are signs posted everywhere that they don't serve ketchup. One time I asked for ketchup as a joke. No one laughed. I am opposed to prejudice in any form, including condiment snobbery. These people are *antiketchupists*. They don't even have ketchup in little packets for the fries. *They oughtta be arrested.*

You can't deny the taste of the food here though. The hot dogs are the old style with the skin still on, so they snap a little when you bite into them. At Jimmy's, "everything on it" means mustard, onion, relish, and peppers by request. The Polish sausage is just as good and a little more filling. The fries though, now there's something special. I don't know what they do to the oil to make their fries taste and smell the way they do, but you can't mistake them for any fries anywhere else. Even years after

I stopped working on the West Side, I still recognize that smell in an instant. They are fresh cut every day—they have fifty-five gallon drums full of them—and they constantly cook them, so they're always fresh. The prices are cheap. You can be in and out in less than five minutes. You can also stand at the counter by the window and eat there while you watch the ebb and flow of the West Side neighborhood around you. On any given visit you will see every kind of person you could imagine from poor to rich, every ethnicity, every color, every ironic hairstyle. One time I saw a biker, a priest, a woman in a fur coat, and a drug dealer I'd arrested the week prior. There was no trouble, which led me to believe that if we could just get the Taliban and the French to get together for a hot dog at Jimmy's, we could have peace in our time.

The Dining Room at Kendall College

900 N. Branch St.

866-667-3344

culinary.kendall.edu/news-and-events/the-dining-room/

Cuisine: *student gourmet*

Kendall College is Chicago's best-known culinary school. They have a kitchen in which students practice their craft. What to do with all the food? Sell it of course. When I was a kid, my mom saved money by taking us to the barber school for cheap haircuts and the dental school for cheap dentistry (that didn't work out so well). So when I heard that Kendall had a student kitchen, I had to try it out.

Actually, there are two restaurants in Kendall. They serve breakfast and lunch in the cheap one for about $5. The other restaurant serves gourmet dinners and is a really nice place. The prices are around $40 for dinner, but it's for meals by chefs that will be working in kitchens that will charge $100 for a teaspoonful of braised carrots someday. The menu changes daily. I've never had a bad meal there and have tried some things I would never order in a regular restaurant.

The kitchen is run by an instructor, and the students do the actual preparation of the food. These kids are working for grades, so they work hard.

If you eat in the main restaurant off duty, it's BYOB, with a $15 corkage fee. This is the kind of place where the kids show up the next day and say, "Hey, some guy ate my homework."

Manny's Deli

1141 S. Jefferson
312-939-2855
www.mannysdeli.com
Cuisine: *corned beef*

Manny's is a famous old Chicago place that has the best corned beef anywhere. Although it's pretty expensive by local lunch standards, Manny's corned beef is definitely worth trying when your pockets are full on payday. Plus, you might run into somebody you've seen on TV. Daley has even had his birthday party here.

Be very specific when you order. The first time I ate at Manny's was on midnights in the 001 District. It was early in the morning, and I went there for breakfast. I'd heard about their corned beef, so instead of getting bacon or sausage with my eggs, I asked for corned beef instead. They must have misunderstood, because they came out with about a pound of corned beef. It was really good, but I had to take most of it home.

In addition to corned beef, Manny's has a substantial lunch menu, and they recently began staying open for dinner. They even do catering.

For lunch, they have five or six specials, including oxtail stew on Thursdays. They have both hot and cold sandwiches and salads. Along with that, they have a lot of Jewish specialties like potato pancakes, knishes, and herring. I have not tried the herring, and never will, but I hear it's good.

Manny's has been around since 1942, and has all kinds of clippings on the walls showing the history of the restaurant, and the history of the last fifty years of Chicago.

Manny's is located just north of Roosevelt, on Jefferson. That's around the corner from where the Maxwell Street market is on Sunday mornings. The Maxwell Street market is nothing compared to what it used to be in the old days, but it is still a pretty cool place to go on a Sunday morning. Check it out right before lunch at Manny's.

The Original Mitchell's
1953 N. Clybourn Ave.
773-883-1157
Cuisine: *breakfast*

The Original Mitchell's doesn't only serve breakfast, it's just that of all the times I've eaten there, the breakfast was the one thing I found to be truly exceptional. Not that anything else was bad, but the breakfast was *so good*.

There are several Mitchell's around the city. I recommend the Mitchell's on Clybourn because the prices seem more in line with what normal people pay. I've been to the two downtown locations, and the food was good, but when the bill came, it ruined all of the wonderful feelings that come with a good breakfast.

When you work midnights, eating is a hard thing. You can eat between midnight and 2:00 a.m. but then you have to spend the next six hours full and dopey. There is nothing really good open between two and five. So then you have breakfast places, and by then you are usually ravenous or too sleepy to eat. I've met some people who completely reverse their eating lifestyle. They eat dinner at 9:00 or 10:00 a.m., breakfast around dinnertime, and they bring a lunch to work. They will then eat their lunch halfway through their shift at midnight. If you can get on a schedule like that, it's probably the easiest. You should not have a spouse or kids, or else you would rapidly lose both.

Mitchell's breakfast is not gourmet fancy, but they do it very well. When you say that you want eggs with the whites cooked but the yolks soft, it comes that way. That alone would make me come back. The service is very pleasant, and the food is prepared quickly and served hot. The décor of the place is reminiscent of old diners and makes you feel like a kid out for breakfast after church. It's relaxing and feels safe.

Moon's Sandwich Shop
16 S. Western Ave.
773-226-5094
moons.homestead.com
Cuisine: *breakfast, sandwiches, breakfast sandwiches*

Reminiscent of the lunch counters of the last century, Moon's looks probably the same as it did when it opened in 1933. Located at Madison and Western, Moon's has been a fixture in a neighborhood that has gone from good to ghetto and is on its way back to good again. Gentrification has begun on the West Side. It remains to be seen if Moon's will be able to stay a part of this vibrant part of Chicago.

Among police and city workers, Moon's is famous for its breakfast sandwiches. Served on white or wheat toast, with cheese, fried egg, and choice of meat, it's the best quick meal for people on the run.

If you have time to sit down for a while, you will see a cross section of Chicago's citizenry, from people just leaving a late-night bar to garbage men right before they start their route. Jimmy Radek, the owner, was a police officer right there in the Filmore District until he quit in 1979 to take over Moon's. A police officer is the best source for food that police officers like.

Palace Grill
1408 W. Madison Ave.
312-226-9529
Cuisine: *breakfast, diner*

Another famous place with a great breakfast and the rest of their menu's not bad either. When I say famous, I mean famous people eat there. There are tons of celebrities' pictures on the walls. The Palace is located across the street from Johnny's Ice House, and across the street from Chicago's 911 center. Many of Chicago's political and hockey elite eat at the Palace.

One of the great things about eating at local joints is when the owner is loud, vocal, and knows who you are. George greets everyone who comes in. He tells jokes, makes wisecrack comments, yells orders, and generally keeps the energy of the place up high. The fact that he knows so many of the people packed into the place on a Sunday morning is a testament to diners' tendency to come back again and again.

The lunches are huge and delicious. Even a beat cop can find himself carrying a bag full of meatloaf and mashed potatoes back to the squad car. But let me get back to breakfast. Giant. Steaming. Wonderful. The omelets must have seventeen eggs each. They're titanic pillows of yellow goodness stuffed to exploding with ham, green onions, bacon, and cheese (if you ordered the Denver, which they claim is the best in the world). The Palace is one of those local places people from out of town know about, a legendary grill on par with Manny's for its impact on Chicago local cuisine. It's a destination grill. The kind of place you bring your visiting relatives just to watch them push their fat ass away from the table and declare, "Enough, enough."

A caveat: be prepared on weekends and especially on Sundays to stand in line and to be jostled, pleasantly, by people wide-eyed and drooling trying not to eat all their food before they get to their table. If there's a table.

Ricobene's
252 W. 26th St.
312-225-5555
www.ricobenesfamoussteaks.com
Cuisine: *breaded steak*

Probably one of the safest places in the city to eat. I cannot recall a single time when I was in there and I wasn't among other police officers. Ricobene's is famous for its breaded steak sandwich, which only the largest street and san man could finish in one sitting. Luckily most city workers, except police, take more than one lunch in a given day.

The sandwich that made Ricobene's famous is a thin steak, breaded and deep fried, served on crusty bread with Italian red gravy. I've talked about gigantic sandwiches elsewhere in this book, and you've heard your friends tell you about some place where they couldn't finish their plate. We all exaggerate about this all the time. Not at Ricobene's. You remember the *Flintstones* opening when they served a rack of brontosaurus ribs and his car tipped over? It's kind of like that, only bigger. You will not finish this sandwich. You will try. You will claw and rend your way through its crispy, red-saucy, deep-fried breaded steak, toothy gastroeuphoric paradise of grease and artery-clogging sandwich divinity but you won't make it. EMTs will have to come in with the jaws of life and pry your carcass out of your wrecked dinner. They should serve these sandwiches with a defibrillator and a priest. They should take your order and ask for your next of kin.

I work on the North Side of the city. The headquarters building is on the South Side, near where a bunch of hooligans gather to pretend to be a major-league baseball team. It is a pain in the ass for someone to go from where I work down to headquarters. The average police officer tries to avoid it; sometimes however, people have to go there. Every once in a while, I get to tell someone that their name came up to take a random drug test.

When a police officer's name comes up in the computer (it really is random) then the drug test unit calls the desk sergeant in the district, gives them a name, and tells them to have the officer down there by ten in the morning. They usually call by six, and the officer usually starts at seven or eight. As soon as I get the notification, I have to fill out a form, which the officer has to bring down with him. I love when this happens, and to make a short story long, when I give the officer the form, it is often accompanied with a order for Ricobene's and some money. Don't worry, I buy her lunch too.

After the breaded steak, Ricobene's is locally hailed for their delicious pizza and their chicken vesuvio, a dish that should be praised in Wisconsin for its singular ability to keep their dairy industry alive on its butter content alone. Did we mention this isn't a diet book?

The dining room is black and white tile and looks like someone called a Hollywood studio to order a set that looks like a Chicago restaurant from the 1930s, Capone headshots and all. And we're not kidding about the cops. They should just move the precinct headquarters to Ricobene's and save gas.

Finally, don't make a rookie mistake: it's pronounced "Rick O' Benny's," not "Rice O' Beans," a mistake our illustrious co-author can assure you is not safe to make in the company of seasoned beat cops who've been off duty in a bar for more than five minutes. Trust me, haranguing will occur.

Union Park

228 S. Racine Ave.

312-243-9002

www.unionparkchicago.com

Cuisine: *yuppy sandwiches*

The restaurant that used to stand on the site of Union Park was called the Racine Café. For many years, generations of police officers went through the police academy, located a block away, and walked down to the Racine Café for lunch. The Racine Café joins a list of restaurants that are gone now, but live on in the minds of police officers in Chicago.

The owners of Union Park could've paid homage to the memory of the Racine Café by creating a run-down restaurant with bland food at high prices. Instead, the Union Park people gutted the building. Now it's a very nice sports pub with a full bar that serves first-class food including excellent pub grub, soups from scratch, and the rare, delicious, sweet potato fries.

All the tables are surrounded by large flat-screen TVs, and sports are always on. These days, since the neighborhood is gentrifying, the prices are a little high for your average police officer to go there often. And you are most likely to see older officers than young recruits these days.

It's no longer a greasy spoon, and it's no longer a place to hang out and study traffic laws and report writing, but the food is good, and the memories of what it used to be are locked in my head.

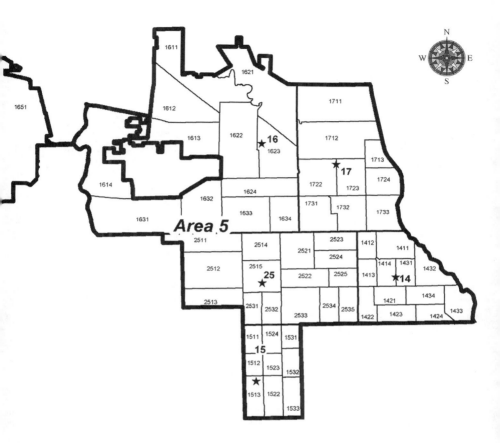

"The scientific name for an animal
that doesn't either run from or fight its
enemies is lunch."
—Michael Friedman

Alice's Restaurant

5638 W. Chicago Ave.
773-921-1100
Cuisine: *soul*

Alice's restaurant is a West Side icon. When I worked in the fifteenth, I would go on Sunday mornings for breakfast. Although they have a full menu, their breakfast is first rate. The restaurant doesn't look like much from the outside, and on the inside, it looks a little shabby as well. The staff is cop friendly and the food is cheap. They serve biscuits and gravy, eggs any way you want, and potatoes. (Sundays will be very busy with the church crowd.)

Alice's is iconic because their food is delicious. But, also, because they serve a Chicago South Side staple: soul food. Most North Siders didn't know Chicago had great soul food until they watched Aretha Franklin demand some respect in *The Blues Brothers*, from Lyon's Deli on Maxwell Street. But Chicago's special relationship with the *South* is as old as the city itself and certainly can be traced back to the Civil War displacement of African Americans who brought their families north, settled down, and started cooking. And thank God they did.

There aren't many cities north of the Mason-Dixon Line where you can confidently eat soul food without wanting to throw a cast iron pot through the window after your first bite. The deft execution of navy beans, mustard greens, and cornbread is every bit as complicated and demanding as frying chicken or cooking oxtail soup and deserves respect. Alice's serves up a plate of soul as southern as any you'll get in Alabama. It does a body proud. In particular, their insistence on black-eyed peas and navy beans just proves their gustatorial heritage as perfectly authentic.

Except for one horrendous, unforgivable, feud startin' whopping hole in the ground that makes Alice's plumb crazy: they don't serve banana pudding. They serve rice pudding. It's delicious, no complaints, but if you're a displaced Alabama mama's boy with a gutwrenching ache for true soul food, topping off the best homecooked meal in Chicago, a platter spilling over with greens, cornbread, oxtail, fried chicken, and everything else you could order, with *rice* pudding at the end is just a hideous reminder that you're that far away from home.

Flash Taco

1570 N. Damen Ave.
773-772-1997
www.flashtacobucktown.com
Cuisine: *tacos*

Chicago can often let you down when you're hungry after hours. Chicago is the city that works, so it has to get a good night's rest. If you're hungry after 10:00 p.m., you can find yourself choosing between a sandwich from White Hen or McDonald's. Unless you're in Wicker Park—then you eat at Flash Taco and you thank God they're there. Ten years ago, *Metropolis* magazine listed Wicker Park as one of the top 100 coolest neighborhoods in America, and it's only gotten better. As far as I'm concerned, Flash Taco is the center of the Wicker Park nanoverse, the very best place to grab a quick taco or a couple of flautas.

Flash Taco is small. Late at night, they're full of well-heeled drunks coming out of the Double Door and other local clubs. But they're usually highly literate drunks and unless you're a cop on duty, you're probably going to be a local club drunk too. The menu is typical Mex-American over-the-counter fast food—they're called Flash Taco for a reason. Ultimately, they're not breaking any new ground with their food. Their tacos are really good but they're just tacos. I like them for their torta Cubana, the Cuban sandwich.

A good Cuban is a thing to behold. Like all great food, it's simple. Direct. Just ham, pickles, mustard, mayo, and queso blanco between two crumbly slices of French bread, pressed in a hot grill till it's all melted and flat. But man oh man when you've been out drinki—um, on patrol late at night and you're starving to death, there's just nothing like it. For added authenticity, get a bottle of Jaritos Tamarindo soda.

StreetWise

Johnnie's on North Avenue in Elmwood Park has the best Italian beef and sausage combo in Chicago because Johnnie's cooks everything over charcoal. Get the combo, extra juicy with sweet peppers. This, my friend, is the greatest sandwich in history. The smell of Johnnie's is enough to draw you in—you can smell the charcoal from blocks away. The smell of that place alone completely separates their beef from Al's on Taylor, Tony's on Pulaski, or Portillo's, or anywhere else for that matter. Don't even bother getting something to drink. Instead, get a large lemon Italian ice to help wash your combo beef and sausage down. This is the second best Italian ice, second only to Freddie's on 31st and Union. Eating a combo and Italian ice at Johnnie's on a hot, humid July evening almost makes going back to work in nearby 025 or 015 tolerable. Well, not quite, but at least you ate well before your next foot chase!

—P. O. Robert "Fiber" K.

Bill's Drive-In

5729 N. Northwest Highway

773-775-2035

Cuisine: *drive-in food*

Bill's Drive-In is at the corner of Nagle and Northwest Highway. It's a classic greasy spoon. They serve your basic breakfast and hot dog stand lunches. The prices are cheap and the food is quick. Just the thing when the inspector's breathing down your neck and you have to stick to a half-hour beat cop's lunch.

Police officers, by contract, get a half-hour lunch and two fifteen-minute personals per day. In theory, a police officer is considered off duty during lunch and does not get paid for it. Still, if someone walks up to you while you're eating lunch to ask you a question, it would be pretty rude to say, "Sorry, I'm off duty, come back later."

In Chicago, the police department has a group of police officers holding the rank of inspector who patrol the city looking for police cars, and making sure they are not violating the general orders of the police department. Punishments range from a "reprimand" to a suspension. One of the things police officers look for in a restaurant is how fast they get the food to the table, so that the officer can finish eating within the half hour.

During the school year when nearby Taft High School lets out in the afternoons, Bill's gets a little crowded with kids, but that doesn't last too long. Bill's is a few blocks away from Norwood Park, which is a nice place to walk off your lunch

A couple of years ago, there was a shoot-out in the parking lot at Bill's Drive-In. An undercover narcotics officer attempted to buy drugs. The dealer suspected he was a police officer and attempted to run over him in his car. The officer fired a couple of rounds before jumping onto a garbage can. The drug dealer was caught five blocks away and is still in prison.

Chikago Pizzaria

6149 N. Milwaukee Ave.
773-631-4111
Cuisine: *pizza*

Despite the weird spelling, Chikago boasts a good Chicago stuffed pizza. Most of the time I get it delivered, but you can also eat in. When police officers decide to get a stuffed pizza for dinner when they are out working the street, they call the order in or stop by and place their order at the restaurant, then go back on patrol until the pizza is ready. Then they can come back in and sit right down and eat. Most of the police-friendly places do this. I've been in situations when other customers complain that the police are getting preferential treatment because they get their food first. Oh well.

Most really good pizza has either really good crust or really good sauce. Sometimes, rarely, they have both. Toppings from one pizza place to the next are usually the same (with rare exceptions like Lou Malnati's).

Chikago's pizza has really good sauce. It's that thick, mildly spicy pizza sauce that sticks to everything. It's hell in a squad car, but I don't care. I love their sauce.

Di Vita's Restaurant
3753 W. Belmont Ave.

773-588-5868

Cuisine: *Italian-American*

Di Vita's is one of those little Italian joints that I've only seen in Chicago. The food is fantastic—almost gourmet. The prices are a little high for police officers to go there often, but on those nights when you're tired of fast food and you have a few dollars in your pocket, or you made a good arrest and your sergeant is springing for dinner, this is the place to go.

I can never figure out what makes some Italian food divine when others are mundane. Whatever that mojo is, Di Vita's has it. Their veal parmigiana is fantastic. They also have great pasta, and the clams are good too. The food takes a little longer to prepare, but it's worth the wait.

Di Vita's is only open at night, so only third-watch cops can go there. But still, it's good for a dinner place. It's also very small and cozy, so it's a good place to take the wife on date night.

Frank and Mary's Tavern

2902 N. Elston Ave.

773-463-8179

Cuisine: *various*

Frank and Mary's was introduced to me by Detective Richard Zuley, who I used to work with. I must have driven by it a million times without knowing it was there. From the outside it looks like an abandoned building. The inside looks like a set from *The Untouchables*. It's an old-style bar: dark wood and dark lighting. You can easily visualize the sawdust on the floor and the smoke of bygone days before the politicians in Illinois decided to make our bars more healthy.

Frank and Mary are brother and sister, and you immediately feel like you are stopping for lunch at a family place. Also, if you don't clean your plate, you'll definitely hear about it from Mary.

Each day they have a soup and two entrées. If you can't decide between the two, you get a plate with half of each, no problem. The food is the type of comfort food from the old days—pot roast, meatloaf, and chicken. They will serve you right at the bar, but they do have a few tables.

The prices are right, and the atmosphere is great. If you can take a few hours on the end (see **Cop Talk**, below), there's no better way than to go for lunch and while away the afternoon watching the Cubs on TV and having a few beers.

▼ COP TALK ▼

When Chicago police officers work overtime, we have the option of getting paid for it, or saving it to use later. Most officers try to have enough hours on the books to take some time off if necessary. When we take time we can either take a day off, or take some time at the beginning of the shift (on the front) or at the end (on the end) of a shift.

Hagen's Fish Market

5635 W. Montrose Ave.

773-283-1944

www.hagensfishmarket.com

Cuisine: *smoked fish*

I'm always amazed when I mention Hagen's to people in my neighborhood and they've never heard of it.

Hagen's has been smoking fish for over sixty years at Central and Montrose in Portage Park. For a $1.75 per pound, they'll hang your freshly caught fish in their cinderblock smokehouse and return them to you, transformed by the alchemy of oak smoke and gravity, into a divine treat.

What I love about Hagen's is the fried shrimp cooked while you wait. I always wonder if shrimp are aware that some quirk of fate made them delicious and if they are pissed about that.

The store is dominated by the cooler loaded with shrimp and fish that you order by the pound. They fry it up and you get it in a paper bag, along with the sauce of your choice. There are no tables at Hagen's—it's all take out. If you're on a beat, you have to sit out in the squad car in the parking lot and eat.

The prices for the shrimp are about the same as what they are in a grocery store, and they change all the time. But they're worth it. If you're going to spend the money, might as well get good, really fresh shrimp.

The dazzling selection of freshly caught smoked fish may cause lesser humans to swoon. The smoked salmon steaks have been known to cause hearty New Englanders to kick themselves in the Chesapeakes for not moving to Portage Park so they can get some real fish. But the telling detail, the simple little truth that makes Hagen's world class, is their hush puppies. Just as any great southern joint must be judged not by its fried chicken but its slaw, any good fish joint must be judged on the delicate tooth, the humid interior, the flaky, cakey, achy-breaky delight of its

Southern Banana Pudding

When I was in the Marine Corps, I only had KP duty one time. During that time I learned how to make banana pudding. I also learned how to make "shit on a shingle" (corned beef hash on toast) but my father is the only person I know who likes that, so I didn't add it to the book. The recipe for banana pudding that I learned is basic. And if you read the review of MacArthur's restaurant in this book, you know that somehow, someway this recipe can be better. However, this is the way I make it.

¾ cup granulated sugar
½ cup flour
A little salt (dash)
4 eggs (whites and yolks separated, ask your wife how to do that)
2 cups of milk
½ teaspoon vanilla (I add a little more)
At least one box of Nilla Wafers (buy two if you have kids, because they will eat half of what you buy, unless you have an unusual measure of control)
6 bananas

Combine ½ cup sugar, flour, and salt in top of double boiler. Stir in 4 egg yolks and milk and blend well. Cook, uncovered, over boiling water, stirring constantly until thickened. Turn the heat down and continue cooking, stirring for about five minutes. Turn the heat off, and add vanilla. Spread a small amount on the bottom of 1½ quart casserole pan; cover with a layer of Nilla Wafers, then a layer of sliced bananas. Spoon some more of the pudding mixture over the bananas, followed by a layer of wafers, then bananas. Continue until all of the pudding mixture is used up. Allow to cool for 30 minutes. Top with Cool Whip or whipped cream.

(This recipe receives Mr. Garlington's stamp of approval for southern authenticity. It's delicious and done right, just like mama used to make.)

hush puppies. Hagen's hush puppies are so frightfully superior, so addictively delicious, you will forget you came there to get some fish. Having scoured this great country in search of the best hush puppies around, I can confidently claim only Jacque Imo's in New Orleans can boast a better pup—and they had to add garlic, alligator, and crawdaddies to get past Hagen's hush puppies.

(Note: as this book nears publication, Hagen's just started offering smoked salmon candy. Words fail me. What sanguine grace causes a person to look at smoked salmon and brown sugar and think: this'll work? There's a special place in heaven for them and when I die? That's where I'll eat.)

Hot Doug's

3324 N. California Ave.
773-279-9550
www.hotdougs.com
Cuisine: *encased meats*

Encased meats is a phrase that was especially invented for Hot Doug's. It's not just hot dogs or Polish sausages (although you can get those), but a gourmet meal in a tube. Hot Doug's came to prominence in my neighborhood during a time when Chicago, having solved all of the other problems facing society, decided to go on a crusade to be nice to geese.

Hot Doug's had an item on the menu that was billed as a sausage containing fois gras, which was promptly taken down after the law was passed. Some local reporter wrote about it and the place took off.

These days when I go there, the line at lunch is huge. When I work the desk at my station, we order from there. The menu is on the Internet and their daily specials are updated, well, daily. Each day they have a special game sausage and a type of sausage named after a celebrity. For under ten bucks you can get a sandwich, fries, and drink.

I went there this summer and the line stretched out the door, down the length of the building and across the driveways of two houses. I had an alligator and Cajun rémoulade dog, a blueberry and venison sausage with a brie topping, and an Irish blood sausage named after a celebrity who will surely sue us if we print her name here. I washed it down with a strawberry lime cola.

But Hot Doug's isn't famous merely for the gourmet dogs. They serve the best french fries in the Midwest. Let me repeat that for those of you not paying attention: THE BEST FRIES IN THE MIDWEST!

The fries at Hot Doug's are fried in duck fat which imparts to them, to these pristine slivers of pommes d'or, a delicacy of tooth, a salivate divinity, a taste that is to fries what their Thai chicken dogs are to Oscar Meyer wieners. It is an experience that brings you closer to God and makes you realize, God loves french fries more—a lot more—than ducks.

Duck fat fries are only served on Fridays and Saturdays.

Leo's Cheesecake & Catering

5401 W. Madison St.

773-261-2253

leoscheesecakecatering.blogspot.com

Cuisine: *cheesecake, Southern*

I met Leo when I worked in the Austin District on the West Side of Chicago. I read about this guy who made really good cheesecake and had won a contract supplying it to local casinos.

I had never heard about Leo's at work, and I wondered how a good restaurant had escaped our notice, so I went to investigate.

When I saw his shop I realized how everyone had missed it. Back then, Leo made cheesecakes in a shuttered, run-down former restaurant that he had cleaned up and converted to a cheesecake assembly line. There was a hand-lettered sign out front, but if you didn't look hard, you would miss it. There were no tables, but there were refrigerators, and they sold cheesecake by the slice to walk-in customers.

Over the next couple of years, I got to know Leo and found out that while cheesecake was his main source of income at the time, he was a true chef who wanted to expand.

Eventually, I left the West Side for greener pastures, and when I drove by his place a few months later it was gone. I thought that he had gone out of business.

He hadn't. Leo got his wish and had opened a very nice restaurant on Madison, at the site of the old MacArthur's.

With rosemary ham and smoked turkey on the menu, followed by Leo's now famous cheesecake, Leo's is becoming a West Side icon. And I can say that I knew him way back when.

Off Duty
Riggio's Pizza

7530 W. Oakton St., Niles
847-698-3346
www.riggios.com
Cuisine: *Italian*

When we're not sitting in a car on a stake out, cops spend a lot of time with our families. When we go out, we usually don't take the kids to the same places where we walk our beat. A lot of Chicago cops live in the Northwest neighborhoods (Gladstone Park, Indian Hills, Edgebrook, Sauganash, Edison Park) and take the family out to local places in the adjoining suburbs of Niles, Skokie, and Park Ridge. Of all the great places to eat out there, one of my favorites is Riggio's Pizza.

Don't let the name throw you. Riggio's does serve outstanding pizza (the real stuff), and they deliver, but what they really offer is some of the best family dining outside of Chicago proper.

The Riggios have been running Chicago restaurants for two generations, and every aspect of their operation shows it. From the tasteful and carefully collected art on the walls and the beautiful open-beamed roof, to the careful detail and care given to even the simplest of dishes—their cheese *argentera*—Riggio's radiates a refreshing combination of class and comfort.

 **DETOUR** | # Homer's Ice Cream
1237 Greenbay Rd., Wilmette
847-251-0477 www.homersicecream.com

Ice cream is a big deal in Chicago; even in winter people still go to ice cream shops, and Homer's, though technically not in Chicago, has been a favorite in the city since they cranked out their first batch in 1935. Homer's ice cream descends from that long lost art of making something simple from the very best ingredients. They make it slowly, with the same love and care their founder did sixty years ago. But that's not why they rate a sidebar. Besides being the favorite of North Siders, Homer's was also a favorite of Al Capone. When you sit down in their cozy brick and picnic rooms, wall to wall with hipsters and Little League teams, you got to wonder what flavor Capone would order today?

I'm betting it's not the green tea or the banana macadamia nut crunch. I'm thinking Capone was a classics kind of guy. He would've ordered the Madagascar vanilla, maybe the rocky road, or the spumoni.

Like all great and enduring local joints, Homer's is online. You can have Chicago's best ice cream delivered anywhere in the world.

For the record: Sgt. Haynes gets a three scoop of eggnog, peppermint stick, and maple walnut; Mr. Garlington gets a Baileys and Burgundy cherry malted shake. Why Sgt. Haynes would mix such an ungodly disparity of flavors is either a sign of gastronomic genius or proof his tongue was burned out from too many jalapeño poppers and onion rings. Mr. Garlington's choices indicate a remarkable palate, sanguine distinction, and aplomb.

The Riggios are fanatic foodies with a knack for Chicago authenticity and in the vein of the old-school kitchens like the Cape Cod Room in the bottom of the Drake Hotel, and Twin Anchors rib restaurant that laid the foundation for the foodie mecca Chicago has grown into. Their passion shows in their traditional appetizers, pastas, and Italian platters, all delicately tweaked until they are stellar examples of Italian fare. The baked clams casino, the chicken marsala, and the linguini *fruta di mare fra diavolo* are generously portioned, beautifully presented, and will make you want to pack up and move to Sicily.

The Riggios' lifelong devotion to all things Chicago shows even in their deserts—they use Homer's ice cream, a local purveyor of ice cream since 1935. The spumoni is possibly the best in the city, hands down.

MacArthur's

5412 W. Madison St.
773-261-2316
www.macarthursrestaurant.com
Cuisine: *home cooking*

Mac's is another West Side legend. All the politicians go there, so you'll probably be eating next to an alderman, or maybe even Jesse Jackson, Jr., whom I've seen there once. It's African American cuisine in a classic southern cafeteria style.

I was in the Marine Corps, and Mac's reminds me of eating in the mess halls on Marine bases. I mean that in a good way. In the military, cooks come from all over the country, and somehow their local influences get incorporated into the food. Mac's creates that same effect. I don't understand how or why, but chicken, mashed potatoes, and corn tastes different when it's prepared in a southern, African-American style. The food at Mac's is delicious.

Now to dessert. When I was in the Marine Corps, I had KP duty once, and a Navy cook, a black guy from Louisiana, taught me how to make banana pudding. I still make it sometimes (see recipe on p. 99), and my kids love it, but it doesn't hold a candle to the banana pudding at Mac's.

Papa Joe's

5750 N. Milwaukee Ave.
773-763-4200
www.papajoeschicago.com
Cuisine: *pizza*

There are a million good pizza joints in Chicago. Close to a million. Census figures indicate Chicago boasts over seven thousand places to eat and 6,314 of them serve pizza.[1] All 6,314 of them are somebody's favorite. If there's one kind of food that engenders intractable loyalty, it's the pizza place one takes as one's own. Let's face it; good pizza is not hard to find in Chicago. You can walk blindfolded through most neighborhoods and end up ordering pizza within five minutes. So let's assume 99.99 percent of all Chicago pizzerias serve better than average pie. What matters after that are details. Do they cut it pie or square? Do they use chili flakes or powder? And, most importantly, do they get it there on time without it sticking to the lid of the box?

Papa Joe's pizza is delivered hot; it's ready exactly when they say it will be when I pick it up; they cut square unless you request a pie cut; they know what's going on when you insist that the pepperoni side has a visible blank space where it adjoins the cheese side when you order for the kids; and they're close. When I do order for

---

1 *This is a highly disputable figure derived from Sgt. Haynes and Mr. Garlington's extensive collection of matchbooks and coasters but we're reasonably sure it's pretty dang close to almost exactly maybe the right number.*

delivery, it gets there with cheese still liquid and bubbling.

The prices are fair, and delivery is quick. They can put together a great pizza and have it ready for you if you are on patrol and want to stop in. There's just enough room for two booths.

One of the things I like about Papa Joe's is a little stupid, but endearing. They have an old-fashioned screen door that slams when you go in. Remember that episode of Seinfeld where Kramer got one of those doors for his apartment? They have one at Papa Joe's, and when you go there on a summer night to pick up your pizza, the sound of that door brings back childhood memories, and makes you feel like a kid when getting a pizza was really special.

Paterno's Original Pizza and Sports Bar

5303 N. Milwaukee Ave.

773-631-5522

www.paternopizza.com

Cuisine: *Italian*

Paterno's is a dying breed in Chicago: a neighborhood bar. The bar dominates the place, and most people who go there to sit are there to drink and watch a game. Off in the corner is a counter to order food. If you are not from the Northwest Side of Chicago, you may think that because of the setup, Paterno's is more focused on drinking than food. You'd be wrong. Paterno's makes homemade gourmet Italian food in their small kitchen.

They have a simple dining room, without décorations, next to the bar. If you can, sit in there and have the spaghetti and meatballs. The sauce is a Paterno family tradition. The pizza is great as well, and you can buy some uncooked dough to take home so that the family can have a make-your-own pizza night.

One of the best things they make is called the "incredible"

sandwich. It's an Italian sub, although there are other variations, but the meat and spices and oil make for a great sandwich. To be honest, I'm not sure why this sandwich is so good. I've had a lot of good subs, some of which are listed in this book. I remember the first time I had it, though. I belong to the American Knights Motorcycle Club. It's a club made up of police officers and friends who like riding. One night I stopped in Paterno's with my friend Lucky, who had recently been involved in a shooting a few blocks away while making a drug buy undercover. We were going to have few beers and he was going to tell me about it. We stopped at Paterno's because we wanted some pizza, but unfortunately the kitchen was closed. The owner, Paul, heard us and said that he could make some of these sandwiches. We munched on some "incredibles" and listened to Lucky talk about how the bad guy suspected he was a cop and tried to drive over him. Cops can find humor in any dark situation, and I remember when Lucky described climbing a brick wall trying to avoid getting hit by the bad guy's car after the bullets failed to stop it, I laughed so hard beer came out of my nose. We don't call him Lucky for nothing.

The prices are really good at Paterno's and the service is fast. They don't spend a lot of time on pretension; they just make really good food.

Joe's Barbeque Ribs
5931 W. North Ave.
773-637-0003
Cuisine: *ribs*

Joe's is one of those places you wouldn't go to unless someone told you it's good. It's in a lousy neighborhood, and looks downtrodden, but the food is good—and it's cheap. Chicago in the summer is a cacophony of sights and smells. On those days when it's warm but not oppressive, Chicago is a great place to drive around and look at people. On the West Side, every few blocks you are engulfed by a pillow of the scent of barbeque.

My History Channel addiction prompted me to watch a show about the history of barbeque. They showed pictures of popular barbeque joints in the South during the Jim Crow era. Most of

Lost in Austin

I spent six years of my career roaming the streets of the Austin neighborhood on the West Side of Chicago. I worked every shift, including when on the tactical team, and was there as both a police officer and a field training officer. I saw seven police officers go to jail in the Austin 7 Scandal, and went to two funerals of my coworkers who died in the line of duty there.

In some ways it was the best time of my life. I work now in one of the safest areas in the city, with police officers who are far more experienced and need little supervision—and want even less. There's less of a sense of *esprit de corps* than there was in the old days. My job is much easier, but not nearly as much fun.

Austin had mansions on the west side of the district. The 5900 blocks of Midway Park and Race Streets are some of the most beautiful I've ever seen, and to think that I made dozens of drug arrests within two blocks of there is a staggering thought.

There was a guy who lived on Midway Park who really liked the police. Every summer he would invite all the police over for a picnic. He would give tours of his house. The one thing I remember is that he had a ballroom on the third floor. It was really beautiful. He would set up tables in his yard and we could stop over during our tour of duty and have lunch and ice cream. It was an extremely nice gesture.

Conversely, at the corner of Monroe and Lockwood, the drugs and violence got so bad that for a while we had to assign a car to sit there for weeks at a time.

The best summer I had in Austin was spent doing a foot patrol on Madison Street from 4800–5200 west. My partner, Don Walczak, and I worked from 6:00 p.m. to 2:00 a.m., and most weekend nights we stayed overtime. At that time it was a big hangout—the Rush Street of the West Side. We would walk back and forth, breaking up fights, and moving people along. One night someone sprayed some mace onto the handset of an active pay phone. Everybody who picked up the phone for the next hour got a taste of mace. It was bad for them but funny to watch. I really don't know who sprayed it, but it was the kind of mace cops use.

the really good joints were owned by African-Americans, and most looked like shacks out in the middle of nowhere.

Joe's is a little piece of the South. A shack in the middle of a city, its smoke spreads great barbeque smells throughout the neighborhood.

I remember the first time I went there. I had just met the manager at the hospital the night before. He had gotten into a verbal altercation with his girlfriend. Whatever he said was the wrong thing, and she pulled out a razor and cut him from nose to lip. Really bad.

What struck my partner and I was his attitude. He was sitting there making jokes while the doctor was using what looked like an office stapler to close up his face. He was glad to be alive I guess, and happy that we were going to arrest the girl; plus he was on painkillers, so he was seeing the humor in it all.

When we went to see him a few days later, at work, we tried the food. The humor was gone. After he left the hospital he realized that he couldn't eat ribs for a few months, and that pissed him off more than getting cut. Heaven can be hell if all you can do is look at it.

When you order the rib tips, they come with fries, bread, and great sauce, with a drink, for around five dollars. If you're brave enough to go through the Austin neighborhood, Joe's is worth the stop.

Steers

5777 N. Milwaukee Ave.

773-792-0222

Cuisine: *gyros, hot dogs, cheeseburgers*

An old-style greasy spoon, but with good barbequed ribs and salads too. Steers has something for everyone. The décor is your basic hot dog restaurant, the staff is not very friendly, and the prices are a little high for this Northwest Side neighborhood.

For all their faults, one basic truth remains, the food is great. They deep fry the Polish, and then finish cooking on an open flame. The cheeseburgers are also done over fire. The beef is first rate, and the ribs are essential Chicago style, which means (to aficionados) St. Louis style and dripping with sauce.

The only problem with Steers is the parking lot. Located at the junction of Milwaukee, Austin, and Bryn Mawr in Jefferson Park, the lot is small and the intersection is busy. Add the presence of about six million kids at any given moment from the nearby church and schools, and it makes for very careful driving.

When I used to go to traffic court every month, I had a 016 District copper in my courtroom. Every month he would come to court with about sixty tickets from that corner for people running the red light. He's retired now, but I know that this corner is still a favorite spot for my fellow officers to sit and watch the light.

▼ COP TALK ▼

Just a quick note. Don't try to beat yellow lights in Chicago, especially near schools. Most Chicago police officers, when they need tickets, will sit at lights and stop signs near schools. The reason is most cops hate writing tickets. This may come as a shock to civilians, but it's true. For most cops it makes us feel better to know that at least writing the ticket might have helped save a child. Also it's always easier to write someone who acts like an

a-hole. If you're polite and cooperative, most of the time, you can get off with a warning because the police officer knows that the odds are that the next guy will be rude and uncooperative.

Off Duty
Howard Street Inn
(located at the Tam Golf Course)
6676 W. Howard St., Niles
847-583-0795
www.howardstreetinn.com
Cuisine: *sandwiches*

Golf course restaurants have always been a place to go after, well, golf. You go around the links with your buddies, smoke a couple of good cigars, and repair to the nineteenth hole and celebrate the fact that you kept the score under 150 with a few beers. The Howard Street Inn is one of the few places in this book that's not actually in Chicago, but since Niles is a suburb that is mostly surrounded by the city, Chicago cops do go there.

The best thing about the Howard Street Inn is the atmosphere. The food is good but not extraordinary. The prices are reasonable, even cheap. But what's really great about the place is that it's so relaxing. Looking out the windows, all you see is the golf course, and you feel like you're on vacation. It's also close to the forest preserve bike path, so when you're off duty and not playing golf, it's an ideal place to bike to with the family for lunch.

Taqueria LP Express
4968 N. Elston Ave.
773-282-TACO
pasadita.com
Cuisine: *Mexican*

I love this taco stand because it reminds me of being in Mexico. It's cramped: There's just a counter across the kitchen and a narrow counter under the windows that wouldn't hold six people. It's loud: LaLey FM is blaring Mex-American pop from the kitchen, but there's also a flat screen playing low-budget Mexican action flicks starring all those guys who are bad guys in Quentin Tarantino movies. It sounds like a murder you could dance to. Finally, there are a lot of Mexicans: the crew, the kitchen, the staff, the customers, the guy standing out front hacking the chain off a locked-up bicycle, and the guy in the back who only came out to refill the plastic forks. This is important because in a city with a half a million Mexican Americans looking for street level comfort food, finding a place with a crowd means the food is real.

Taqueria LP Express offers the requisite Chicago taco stand menu with hulking, delicious burritos, Jarito fruit colas, *tortas* (sandwiches), *guisados* (stews), and even *carne asada* (steak). What makes Pasadita stand out is their salsa negra. Made by the proprietor's mother (and the cashier's grandmother) this is salsa verde with the raw ingredients charred. It's more like a chipotle than a serrano or jalapeño salsa. It's smoky, mild, and delicious. I haven't had it anywhere else.

Order the *chachos*, a gigantic plate you might mistake as a nacho plate but it's not. Real nachos don't have beans and meat, just cheese and jalapeños. When you pile it high with beef, beans, queso blanco, and top it off with guacamole and sour cream, that's not nachos. That's *chachos*.

The chorizo taco is by far the best: hot, greasy, spicy, bright-red chorizo; melted cheese; onions; and cilantro wrapped in two corn tortillas (like a real taco). It's three big bites and six or seven napkins worth of taco goodness.

If you're a fan of beef tongue, their *lengua* taco is a real treat, though I prefer it shredded instead of chunked since I still can't quite bring myself to chew something that was recently chewing something.

Tanzitaro

6075 N. Milwaukee Ave.
773-792-1100
www.tanzitaro.com
Cuisine: *Mexican, Guatemalan*

Tanzitaro is a Northwest Side success story. Located at the corner of Elston and Milwaukee, this Mexican diner offers inexpensive, authentic Mexican cuisine in a Mexican setting with Mexicans. Can I say Mexican again?

The owner, Juan Jimenez, grew up in the little town of Tanzitaro in the mountainous Michoacan region of Mexico. The mountains painted on the walls of his restaurant are the mountains he grew up looking at. Juan was a manager for Lettuce Entertain You here in Chicago for many years before stepping out on his own. From the first day he bought what used to be a struggling little Mexican café, Juan has worked tirelessly to turn it into the premiere Mexican restaurant in Jefferson Park and perhaps on the Northwest Side.

My favorite meal at Tanzitaro is the *bistec nopalitos*—steak with baby cactus. I'd never even heard of *nopalitos* before I had them at the Tanz. Now I'm a convert. *Nopalitos* are the tender lobes of a baby cactus sliced into strips. They look kind of like sliced bell pepper until you taste them. They are deliciously tart and, at the risk of sounding too fern bar, they taste green. They're a perfect foil to the slightly charred skirt steak they're served on top of. I don't even talk when I eat them.

My wife thinks I'm insane and wouldn't eat a baby cactus if she was gaunt and dying. For her there is only one dish at the Tanz, the flautas. Again, a dish I never really paid attention to in other places. I always thought they looked suspiciously like taquitos. But my wife ordered them and we ended up fighting for the last piece.

The true test of a local Mexican restaurant, really, is their guacamole. As I am the Guilded Grande Gourmande of Guacamole (see recipe), I will happily heap snobbish derision on wimpy guac. DO NOT serve me anything with mayonnaise in it or I will throw it against the wall; do not serve me a bowl of pasty, glossy, glurp that looks like something you'd serve to Shrek. I want my guac chunky, garlicky, bright, tart, and made thirteen seconds before you served it to me. I want you to still be stirring it at the table. In fact why the hell don't they make guac tableside like they do Caesar salad? Well, the guac at the Tanz measures up. I don't know how Juan finds such perfect avacados—even out of season. He must have a team of avacado pros flying around the world like vegetable spies, FedExing perfectly green, knobbly fruit right from the limbs. However he does it, Juan never runs out and every plate is served with a bright chartreuse crescent lying on the plate, or a bowl of numinous, verdant ambrosia which will send you directly into gastroeuphoria.

One other thing that makes the Tanz the best is Juan and his people. Juan is a gregarious, hilarious, and a generous host. Juan's crew are as gregarious and thoughtful as he is—they remember you, they remember what you like, and they treat you like a visiting dignitary. Juan radiates joy, a love for all things edible, and displays obvious affection for his customers, whose pictures décorate every square inch of his restaurant walls. I don't mean cheap Polaroids either. When Juan takes your picture, you can expect a glossy 8 x 10 framed on the wall within a week. He works a kind of personal magic on his customers; he becomes some kind of confider, a Dutch uncle, and makes you feel like you discovered his restaurant before all of your friends did. I know he does this because even though I discovered Tanz before any of my friends and then E-MAILED THEM AND TOLD THEM ALL ABOUT THE PLACE AND THAT THEY OUGHT TO GO THERE LIKE THREE MONTHS BEFORE THEY SAID WORD ONE ABOUT IT, they all tell me about this place they found, tell me they're such good friends with Juan, or that they want me to have lunch at their place. Bunch of plebes.

Off Duty
Chief O'Neill's Pub & Restaurant
3471 N. Elston Ave.
773-583-3066
www.chiefoneillspub.com
Cuisine: *Irish*

An Irish pub named after an Irish cop—you got to love Chief O'Neill's. Before I get to the food and the beer, I have to explain something. A lot of people see the sign at Chief O'Neill's and make the mistake of believing it's owned by a retired cop. The pub is actually owned by Brendan and Colleen McKinney, two musicians with an enduring passion for traditional Irish music. Brendan plays the Uilleann pipes, the more lyrical and beautiful of the bagpipe twins. We've all heard the Scottish bagpipes, the blowhards of the family, the loud trumpeters of police funerals and the stirring leaders of ancient warriors marching to their deaths in the Scottish Highlands. Here's a generous description of the sound of Scottish bagpipes: imagine an alley cat fighting a chainsaw in a trashcan strapped to the back of a flatbed truck that just shot off the edge of a cliff with its horn blaring.

The Uilleann, or Irish pipes, however, are the sexy longhaired cousin of the Scottish pipes. They're melodious, soft, and mysterious. More importantly, the Irish pipes can play more than two notes so their songs are easy on the ears.

The bar was named after an Irish cop from Chicago, who was a musician and tireless cataloger of Irish folksongs. Chief O'Neill published a number of music books and played all over Chicago. The music calendar at O'Neill's reflects that tireless dedication to great Irish folk music.

The food reflects a real dedication on the part of the McKinneys to offer the very best of classic Irish chow: bangers and mash, Irish stew, fish and chips, Galway Bay mussels, crab cakes, and a great corned beef sandwich. Their food is perfectly prepared and though it is classic, it's not typical, but remains head and shoulders above most pub food I've had in Chicago. Two of their dishes deserve special attention, however.

First: Celtic chili. If there was ever an unlikely pairing, it's Mexican and Irish food. Like English and Welsh fare, Irish food tends toward the meat and potatoes end of the scale with very little spice. In fact no spice. At all. Ever. Celtic food is the polar opposite of Tex Mex and pairing the two is somehow a perversion of fusion cuisine, like having gefilte fish gumbo or Pacific Rim liverwurst. Some things you just don't do. But, you can't judge a chili by its unholy sobriquet, and after steeling myself for something morbid, I was pleasantly surprised.

The second thing is not endemic to Chief O'Neill's but is a standard in true Irish pubs everywhere and that is curry fries. If ever a food was created specifically to pacify the wobbly, sardonic drunkard, it has to be curry fries. And here you have exactly what I said you couldn't do with Celtic food—marry it to a spicy bride. Curry fries are stout potato planks, deep fried, then served slathered in a rich, spicy Indian curry. Sounds insane, I know, but it is delicious and quickly addictive, especially after a couple (of hundred) Guinness pints. You know you're in a good Irish bar if they're on the menu and they stand as testament that any cuisine can be improved. I mean, chips, the deep-fried potato wedges that go so well with deep-fried cod are delicious in their own right, but adding the weird, sweet-spicy tongue of curry just makes them that much better.

West Suburban Hospital Cafeteria

3 Erie Ct., Oak Park
708-383-6200
Cuisine: *hospital cafeteria*

Technically West Suburban is in Oak Park, but for all practical purposes, it's in Chicago. When a police report needs to be done for a patient at West Sub, the hospital calls the Chicago Police Department.

Hospital cafeteria food is an interesting thing to a police officer. All police officers have at least one hospital in their district, and most cops spend some time in hospitals (reports, injuries, hitting on nurses, whatever). In days of yore, hospital cafeterias didn't charge police officers, or at the very least, cops paid the employee rate, so the food was cheap. Being in a hospital, the food is healthy, or close to the emergency room, so either way you know you'll be OK.

West Suburban Hospital's food is as good as any other hospital's cuisine, and a good place to eat. What makes them stand out from other hospitals is the salad bar. They were the first that I know of to have a full-on self-serve salad bar, and it seems to be a point of pride to them. It's always fresh, always delicious, and pretty cheap. There are also main entrées that change every day. Like with most hospitals, they have a make-your-own sandwich bar, plus hot dogs and hamburgers.

Edison Park

It's the farthest west in Chicago you can live and still work for the city, so Edison Park is full of cops, firemen, and city workers— and great restaurants. Maybe it's the proximity to wealthy Park Ridge or maybe it's just natural and organic growth, but over the years, Edison Park has quietly become a bustling home to excellent cafés, sandwich shops, bars, and steak houses. I've eaten wonderful meals at all the restaurants mentioned below, but they are not the sum total of all good places in EP. It's a lovely little Northwest Side neighborhood to explore.

My favorite EP joint has to be **Don Juan Restaurante** (6730 N. Northwest Hwy., 773-775-6438), a Mexican restaurant that is actually two restaurants for reasons I cannot and never will understand. First off, let me tell you that Juan's serves my favorite Mexican appetizer, Duck taquitos. They are served with a salty-sweet corn hash and are absolutely perfect. They also make margaritas with Mescale, a version of tequila with a slightly muskier flavor and more alcohol. The rest of their menu is equal to the taquitos and the atmosphere is bright, cheerful, and upscale.

But here's the weird thing—they have two restaurants. Next to Don Juan's is **Patricio** (6730 N. Northwest Hwy., 773-775-6438), a small, very quiet room with white cloth-covered tables and a separate menu, which has some of the same items as Don Juan's and is cooked in the same kitchen. If you want to eat at Patricio, you tell the maître d' who will walk you through the kitchen to be seated. It's weird, but not unheard of. Jacque Imo's in New Orleans walks every single customer right through the kitchen. It's cool. Say hi to the cooks.

Elliott's Seafood Grille and Chop House
6690 N. Northwest Hwy.
773-775-5277
White tablecloths, unctuous and professional waiters, quiet, old school, and delicious food. A date place.

Zia's Trattoria
6699 N. Northwest Hwy.
773-775-0808
www.ziaschicago.com
Loud, crowded, dim, and loud. The tables are tiny and the chairs are high. But the food is fantastic.

Moretti's
6727 N. Olmsted Ave.
773-631-1175
www.morettischicago.com
This is a restaurant that sprawls over most of a block on the backside of the strip near the railroad tracks. They are, more or less, a sports bar with huge TVs all over the walls in the three main rooms and bar, but they don't feel like a sports bar (unless the Cubs are playing). Their menu is typical Chicago with a leaning toward Italian. The pizza is perfect, the drinks are strong, and the waitresses are great. My favorite thing is the spare room way in the back. It has a huge fireplace and a huge TV and a HUGE elk's head on the wall.

Tony's Italian Deli
6708 N. Northwest Hwy.
773-631-0055
www.tonysdeliandsubs.com
It's a deli. They make subs. They carry all the important stuff you need for an Italian kitchen. And they make a muffaletta sub the way it's supposed to be made, rich, solid, dripping, and unbeatable—except maybe by their prosciutto sub.

If An Elephant Can Paint
6677 N. Northwest Hwy.
773-467-4595
www.ifanelephantcanpaint.com
Ok, this is not a restaurant. It's a detour within a detour! If you go to Edison Park with your family and you have kids, please take an hour or three to spend at "Elephant," a ceramics craft shop. You've seen these places before, where you pick out a ceramic frog and paint it and they fire it and you come pick it

up and the whole joint is full of garden gnomes. Well Elephant ain't that kind of place. First of all they play really good music. Second, they have all kinds of great projects for adults and kids. I made a set of improbably colored cobalt and chartreuse espresso cups with coffee bean stamps on them and people still ask me where I got them. I say they're imported. Our entire family (cousins, aunts, disgruntled brothers-in-law) goes there and has a great time.

Afterword

By Sgt. David Haynes

Near the end of writing this tome, Chris had an inspiration: let's send an e-mail to all the cops we know asking for a quick war story or two involving restaurants around Chicago. I thought it was a great idea and decided that in addition to my cop friends, I would ask the popular Second City Cop blog at (secondcitycop. blogspot.com) to put our request on their site. They did, and there was a huge response. The stories people sent us are sprinkled throughout the book, but we wanted to address some of the comments that the blog entry engendered.

Chief Maurer said in the foreword that there would be endless debate of what was left out of this book and what should have been left out. Already that debate has begun. The comments included some restaurants we haven't tried (but will soon) and some that were forgotten.

Most of the comments left on the Second City Cop blog were anonymous. Any comment referenced is from an anonymous person unless otherwise stated.

> *"What food is good in a squad car? Oh, Dave can *literally* write the book on that. He always leaves enough evidence behind that we know where he stopped all tour long."*

I think that was intended to be mean, but alas he's right. I spent a lot of time researching this book.

"Jimmy's on Grand and Pulaski would satisfy any greasy polish craving... but the worst to eat in the car unless you want to stink it up real nice for the guys on the next watch... and add a touch of grease to the pdt and steering wheel."

Jimmy's is reviewed in this book, and is one of my favorites. This person is right, the smell will linger for hours and the grease will stay on the wheel for the life of the car. The writer makes reference to the "pdt," which stands for "portable data terminal." It's the computer that cops use in the car to run names and plates.

"And did he write this book on company time?"

The writing was done at home, but a lot of research was done on my lunch break and sometimes in the squad car.

"Laurie's Pizza at Foster/Broadway had everything! Pizza, hot dogs, Polish, etc...They even had a room in back for the police. The 'Circuses' were great too! Knife fights between waitresses (several of whom proudly bore children of coppers), strip shows on Tuesday and Friday in the bar, Uptown at its best! 30 years of 020 Coppers loved that place. Today, the place and the area are a mere shadow of their former urban glory! Laurie's sustained three generations of coppers and Uptown clay people....a true landmark."

Laurie's didn't make this book, but this comment was interesting to me. When I worked in the 20th District, I heard old-timers talking about Laurie's, but nobody went there when I was there. It wasn't very good, at least not to me.

"Dog Stop, 6100 W. Belmont. Great hot dogs and homemade Italian beef sandwiches. And they love the police!"

This comment provoked a lot of debate, but the Dog Stop was not included in this book because I just don't like it. Other people might but I don't. I had a bad experience on my way to the Dog Stop. I had a probationary police officer with me, and we were going to lunch at the smorgasbord on Belmont. When we got there we found it closed. The reason I wanted to go there was because it was right next to the Jade Dragon tattoo parlor, and I wanted to get a price on a new tattoo. I told the PPO that we would go find out how much my tattoo was going to be and then head over to the Dog Stop for lunch. As we exited the Jade Dragon, a black unmarked car pulls up and this little female inspector, leaps out of her car and shouts, "Hold it right there!" She sounded like she was making a drug bust; I actually turned and thought about running. As it turns out, we were several blocks outside of our district, and a couple miles away from the job that I "forgot" to come clear from when I went to lunch. I took a two-day suspension for that and it colored my opinion of the Dog Stop.

"Dave and Chris writing this book? Why does that not surprise me. I mean, LOOK at the two of them."

Now that's just not nice. However, if you would like to look at us, we are available for speaking engagements. Just let us know by visiting our blog at www.beatcopsguide.com.

"The Busy Bee, Damen and North, back in the day. Fresh, homemade food seven days a week. Great pirogues."—38 and Gone

I remember eating at the Busy Bee as a kid with my dad. The last time I ate there, I was working special employment for the CTA. My partner pointed to a guy eating across the room and said, "Hey, there's the Galloping Gourmet." Sure enough, Jeff

Smith was eating at the Busy Bee. He came over and said hello, and was very nice. The next day he got arrested for improper relations with a boy and his career was over. The Busy Bee is gone but not forgotten.

"You couldn't beat the since closed down Golden Shell at 10063 Ave. "N." Only place I knew where dicks from all six areas would meet for Sunday breakfast."

"Mass nurse murderer Richard Speck was staying at the upstairs boarding house after his bloodbath across the Calumet River."
—Det. Gourmet, Ret.

We should do a book about places that are gone but not forgotten.

"Anybody remember the Belden Deli at Clark and Belden? It's been gone forever but it was a 24-hour joint that was high on the list for midnight 018th District coppers."

Recently deceased radio personality, Chicago Eddie Schwartz, used to frequent the place after his overnight radio gig and often picked up coppers lunch tabs, usually without even telling them. Guys would ask for their check and the waitress would just say Eddie paid it on his way out.

"In fairness, Ross Cascio, deceased former owner of Lincoln Park Towing, occasionally did the same."

"Good, FAST service for the Police. They REALLY understood how little time we have for lunch."

Eddie Schwartz was a great guy. Before he got sick I would see him occasionally around the neighborhood. A real Chicago icon who always had a good word for the police. When I worked in the 20th District, I would also run into Studs Terkel, who was a hell of a guy. I once answered a B.S. call on Terkel's block, and he came out to say hello. A real nice guy.

"Any place where your food is free of boogers or other contaminants."

That's the truth! It's also one of cops' biggest fears. When you visit most of the places in this book, you will notice that you will be able to see where they prepare the food.

"On the last few days before payday, we dined at: Lawry's for the prime rib; Chez Paul for the ham sandwich; and Ireland's for the fish sandwich."

A lot of cops who work downtown do eat at good restaurants on payday. These weren't included in the book, however, because they did not meet the under $10 criteria. Another great place that cops eat is hotel cafeterias, but I left them out because most of the time the public does not have free access. I wanted to mention it somewhere though, because when I worked down in the 1st District, I noticed that a lot of the hotels also sent that same food down to the homeless people down on lower Wacker. They did it without fanfare or publicity, and I thought that was nice.

"Taurus on Stony?? Been a while but we remember there were two Taurus Ice Cream/Sandwich shops, one on the 900 block of W. 79th (sad about the copper) and one on the 600 block of E. 79th."

"Sentimental favorite is the one on W. 79th... Had our faces in the place as wee one. The steak hoagie was delish and the double scoop ice cream cone was a treat."

"You guys are bringing back too many memories!!"
—The Box Chevy Phantom

I'm trying to convince the publisher to let me do the next book titled *The Beat Cop's Guide to Chicago Sweets*. My wife's a little leery though. I gained fifty pounds doing this book.

Beat Cop Bucks!

Branko's Submarines
1118 W. Fullerton Ave.
$2 off a minimum
$10 purchase.
Can't be combined
with other offers.
One per customer.

Chief O'Neill's Pub and Restaurant
3471 N. Elston Ave.
$2 off a minimum
$10 purchase.
Can't be combined
with other offers.
One per customer.

Clark Street Dog
3040 N. Clark St.
$2 off a minimum
$10 purchase.
Can't be combined
with other offers.
One per customer.

The Beat Cop's Guide to Chicago Eats

The Beat Cop's Guide to Chicago Eats

The Beat Cop's Guide to Chicago Eats

Flash Taco
1570 N. Damen Ave.
$2 off a minimum
$10 purchase.
Can't be combined
with other offers.
One per customer.

Di Vita's Restaurant
3753 W. Belmont Ave.
$2 off a minimum
$10 purchase.
Can't be combined
with other offers.
One per customer.

Frank and Mary's Tavern
2902 N. Elston Ave.
$2 off a minimum
$10 purchase.
Can't be combined
with other offers.
One per customer.

Gulliver's
2727 W. Howard St.
$2 off a minimum
$10 purchase.
Can't be combined
with other offers.
One per customer.

The Beat Cop's Guide
to Chicago Eats

The Beat Cop's Guide
to Chicago Eats

The Beat Cop's Guide
to Chicago Eats

The Beat Cop's Guide
to Chicago Eats

Hagen's Fish Market
5635 W. Montrose Ave.
$2 off a minimum
$10 purchase.
Can't be combined
with other offers.
One per customer.

Manny's Deli
1141 S. Jefferson
$2 off a minimum
$10 purchase.
Can't be combined
with other offers.
One per customer.

Mexico Steakhouse
2983 S. Archer Ave.
$2 off a minimum
$10 purchase.
Can't be combined
with other offers.
One per customer.

Misericordia
Greenhouse Inn
6300 N. Ridge Ave.
$2 off a minimum
$10 purchase.
Can't be combined
with other offers.
One per customer.

The Beat Cop's Guide to Chicago Eats

The Beat Cop's Guide
to Chicago Eats

The Beat Cop's Guide
to Chicago Eats

The Beat Cop's Guide
to Chicago Eats

Palace Grill
1408 W. Madison Ave.
$2 off a minimum
$10 purchase.
Can't be combined
with other offers.
One per customer.

Papa Joe's
5750 N. Milwaukee Ave.
$2 off a minimum
$10 purchase.
Can't be combined
with other offers.
One per customer.

Spacca Napoli
1769 W. Sunnyside Ave.
$2 off a minimum
$10 purchase.
Can't be combined
with other offers.
One per customer.

Steak & Egger
1174 W. Cermak Rd.
$2 off a minimum
$10 purchase.
Can't be combined
with other offers.
One per customer.

The Beat Cop's Guide to Chicago Eats

The Beat Cop's Guide to Chicago Eats

The Beat Cop's Guide to Chicago Eats

The Beat Cop's Guide to Chicago Eats

Steers
5777 N. Milwaukee Ave
$2 off a minimum
$10 purchase.
Can't be combined
with other offers.
One per customer.

Tropic Island Jerk Chicken
419 E. 79th St.
$2 off a minimum
$10 purchase.
Can't be combined
with other offers.
One per customer.

The Beat Cop's Guide to Chicago Eats

The Beat Cop's Guide to Chicago Eats

Index

Acknowledgments

Special thanks go to a couple of people:
To my wife, Anne Haynes. She's my best friend, my true love, and the only person who could put up with my "Walter Mitty" lifestyle. She's also the only person I know in my life I'm sure is real. Pretty sure anyway . . . ; to Nate, Julia, and Michele; to Scooby, Roon, and Rah; to Second City Cop blog for putting the word out; to Lake Claremont Press for giving us a chance; and to Chief Jim Maurer for the foreword.

Publisher's Credits
Cover design by Timothy Kocher. Interior design and layout by Todd Petersen. Editing by Laurel Haines. Index by Rachael Patrick.

About the Authors

09–344-21 Chicago P.D.
Sgt. David "Biscuit" Haynes

Sgt. David J. "Biscuit" Haynes is a lifelong resident of Chicago, leaving only for four years to serve in the U.S. Marine Corps. Haynes has spent the past 15 years as a proud member of the Chicago Police Department, working some of the toughest neighborhoods on Chicago's West Side, running Chicago's first ever Homeland Security Task Force, and supervising squads in the 19th District at Belmont and Western. He and his wife Anne have three children. Haynes is an Italian beef aficionado, active in ward politics, and smokes a JFR with a Connecticut wrapper. He makes the best chocolate chip cookies ever and has mastered the preparation of all the breakfast foods.

09–344-21 Chicago P.D.
Chris "Bull" Garlington

Christopher "The Bull" Garlington is a blogger and author, known for his stories of raising highly intelligent (devious) children published on the blog Death by Children. His articles have appeared in the *Daily Herald*, the *Chicago Tribune*, *Chicago Parent*, *Orlando Magazine*, *Florida Magazine*, *Exito!*, *Catholic Digest*, and the *Orlando Weekly*. His fiction has appeared in *Another Realm*, *Bathhouse*, *South Lit*, and *The Dead Mule School of Southern Literature*, of which he is most proud. Garlington writes from his home in Chicago. He smokes a La Gloria Cubana Seri R maduro, drinks Belgian ales, and makes a mean Gumbo.

Together Haynes and Garlington have hosted the radio program *The Dave & Chris Show!* since 2007, during which they cultivate and maintain a long-standing argument about…everything. From politics and video games to the importance of cool nicknames and secret societies, they cover it on their live weekly broadcast from cigar stores, bars, and other manly locales around Chicago. Their show first aired on WJJG and is now broadcast online (*http://www.blogtalkradio.com/perfectly-harmless*).

Founded in 1994, **Lake Claremont Press** specializes in books on the Chicago area and its history, focusing on preserving the city's past, exploring its present environment, and cultivating a strong sense of place for the future. Visit us on the Web at www.lakeclaremont.com, on Facebook, and on Twitter (@ChicagoPress).

Selected Booklist

On the Job: Behind the Stars of the Chicago Police Department

Historic Bars of Chicago

A Chicago Tavern: A Goat, a Curse, and the American Dream

Wrigley Field's Last World Series: The Wartime Chicago Cubs and the Pennant of 1945

Finding Your Chicago Irish

Finding Your Chicago Ancestors: A Beginner's Guide to Family History in the City and Cook County

Graveyards of Chicago

For Members Only: A History and Guide to Chicago's Oldest Private Clubs

Rule 53: Capturing Hippies, Spies, Politicians, and Murderers in an American Courtroom

The Politics of Place: A History of Zoning in Chicago

The Chicago River: A Natural and Unnatural History

The Chicago River Architecture Tour

Carless in Chicago

Chicago TV Horror Movie Shows: From Shock Theatre to Svengoolie

The Golden Age of Chicago Children's Television

Hollywood on Lake Michigan: Chicago and the Movies

Michelle L'Amour's Sexy Chicago